The Epistle to

THE HEBREWS

The Epistle to

THE HEBREWS

By

CHARLES F. PFEIFFER

MOODY PRESS

CHICAGO

ISBN: 0-8024-2058-3

NOTE: The author has used the King James Version as his basic English text. In some instances the Greek text itself has been translated by the author, who availed himself of the suggestions made by scholars whose works are cited in the Bibliography. In each instance comparison has been made with other English translations before suggesting a reading.

CONTENTS

CHAPTER   PAGE

Introduction 7

Outline 11

I. The Revelation of God in His Son 15

II. The Faithful Saviour 31

III. The Great High Priest 39

IV. Practical Exhortations 82

Bibliography 125

INTRODUCTION

Who Wrote Hebrews?

THE EPISTLE TO THE HEBREWS is anonymous. The name of Paul was not associated with it until the end of the second century, and even then many other authors were suggested. The early church suggested Barnabas, Luke, Silvanus, Philip, Priscilla, and Clement as possible writers of the letter. Martin Luther suggested still another author—the eloquent Apollos of Alexandria (Acts 18:24, 25). Calvin concluded, "Who, then, composed it is not to be discovered, however hard one labors, but that the nature of the thought, and that the style are quite unlike Paul's is abundantly evidenced." The Spirit of God has seen fit to use numerous unnamed writers in giving us our Bible. Neither external nor internal evidence is sufficient to solve the problem of identifying the author of Hebrews. God spoke through him, however, and his message was designed to edify the Church of Jesus Christ.

When Was the Epistle Written?

Internal evidence indicates that the Epistle to the Hebrews was written before the destruction of Jerusalem (A.D. 70). Since the epistle argues that the death of Christ renders obsolete the Old Testament sacrificial system it seems certain that mention would have been made of the destruction of the Temple if that had already taken place.

The letter makes reference to persecution (12:4) and it implies that Christians had been called upon to suffer much for the cause of Christ. The persecution under Nero came to a head in A.D. 64, and it is probable that the Epistle to the Hebrews was written some time during the decade A.D. 60-70.

From What Place Was It Written?

Although the letter itself contains no hint of its point of origin, Alexandria in Egypt has often been suggested. Alexandria contained a large Jewish settlement which formed something of a synthesis between Judaism and Hellenism. There, during the third and second centuries B.C., the Hebrew Scriptures were translated into Greek in the version known as the Septuagint. The author of Hebrews consistently quotes from that translation. The contrast between the "shadow" of the Old Testament and the heavenly reality which finds its ultimate expression in Christ would be of particular interest to Jews who had an interest in Platonic philosophy, as the Alexandrians did. Philo of Alexandria (25 B.C.-C. A.D. 50) was a leading exponent of Hellenistic Judaism.

To Whom Was the Letter Addressed?

The Epistle "to the Hebrews" was addressed to Jewish Christians. The writer had a particular congregation of believers in mind (cf. 5:11, 12; 6:10, 11; 13:19). We are not certain where they lived—Jerusalem, Caesarea, Ephesus, and Antioch have been suggested. The most probable location, however, is Rome. The epistle was known in Rome as early as A.D. 95 when Clement of Rome quoted it in a letter to the Corinthians. Internal evidence may be found in the words, "they of Italy salute you" (13:24), implying that Christians from Italy living near the writer wished to be remembered to their kinsmen at home.

WHY WAS THE LETTER WRITTEN?

The writer of the Epistle to the Hebrews knew and loved those whom he addressed. They had been true to Christ in past times of persecution. There were, however, signs of defection, and the letter was written to sound a warning against apostasy (6:4-8; 10:26-31; 12:14-19). Refuge could not be sought in the Old Testament economy, which was now antiquated (12:18-29). There must, indeed, be a willingness to press on into spiritual maturity (6:1-3). Christ is God's "last word" to man and, while He may bring trials into the lives of His children, they must learn that the life of faith is the life of divine blessing.

OUTLINE

I. THE REVELATION OF GOD IN HIS SON, 1:1–2:18

    A. Christ the Climax of Revelation, 1:1-3

    B. Christ's Superiority over the Angels, 1:4-14
        1. He is the Son, 1:4-6
        2. His reign is eternal, 1:7-14

    C. The Danger of Neglecting Salvation through the Son, 2:1-4

    D. The Son and Humanity, 2:5-18
        1. Man's lowliness and dignity, 2:5-8
        2. The necessity for the incarnation, 2:9-18
            a. To fulfill God's gracious purpose, 2:9-10
            b. To make one the Saviour and the saved, 2:11-15
            c. To enable the Saviour to sympathize with the saved, 2:16-18

II. THE FAITHFUL SAVIOUR, 3:1–4:13

    A. Christ, as Son, Superior to Moses, as Servant, 3:1-6

    B. Consequences of Israel's Unbelief, 3:7-11

    C. Warning against Unbelief, 3:12-19

    D. Exhortations to Faithfulness, 4:1-13
        1. A rest remains for the people of God, 4:1-11
        2. The omniscient God is judge, 4:12-13

III. THE GREAT HIGH PRIEST, 4:14—10:18
   A. Confidence in Christ's Priesthood, 4:14-16
   B. Christ's Possession of the Essential Qualities for Priesthood, 5:1-10
      1. Sympathy with men, 5:1-3
      2. God's appointment, 5:4-10

   C. Spiritual Dullness of the Hebrews, 5:11—6:12
      1. Lack of growth in knowledge, 5:11-14
      2. Need for pressing on to maturity, 6:1-3
      3. Danger of falling away from Christ, 6:4-8
      4. Hope for better things, 6:9-12

   D. God's Word and Oath, a Ground of Confidence, 6:13-20

   E. Christ, a Priest after the Order of Melchizedek, 7:1-28
      1. The history of Melchizedek, 7:1-3
      2. The superiority of Melchizedek to Aaron, 7:4-10
      3. The Aaronic priesthood superseded by that of Melchizedek, 7:11-19
      4. The superiority of Christ's priesthood, 7:20-24
      5. Christ, the Priest who meets our needs, 7:25-28

   F. Christ the True High Priest, 8:1—10:18
      1. His entrance into the true sanctuary, 8:1-5
      2. Christ as Priest of the New Covenant, 8:6-13
      3. The old Tabernacle and its services, 9:1-7
      4. Ineffectiveness of the sacrifices of the old Tabernacle, 9:8-10
      5. Superiority of Christ's sacrifice, 9:11-14

6. The Mediator of the New Covenant, 9:15-28
7. Weakness of the sacrifices of the Law, 10:1-5
8. The incarnation, 10:6-9
9. The one satisfactory offering, 10:10-18

IV. PRACTICAL EXHORTATIONS, 10:19—13:25

A. Drawing Near to God and Holding Fast the Faith, 10:19-23
B. Christian Responsibility and God's Judgments, 10:24-31
C. Past Faithfulness a Ground for Present Confidence, 10:32-39
D. The Household of Faith, 11:1-40
   1. Characteristics of faith, 11:1-3
   2. Examples of faith, 11:4-32
   3. Triumphs of faith, 11:33-40
E. Running the Race, 12:1-3
F. Sufferings as Discipline, 12:4-11
G. Duties toward the Brethren, 12:12-17
H. The Two Covenants, 12:18-29
I. Christian Duties, 13:1-17
   1. Moral and social relations, 13:1-6
   2. Loyalty to leaders in the Church, 13:7-8
   3. Warning against heresies, 13:9-14
   4. Life in the church, 13:15-17
J. Personal Matters, 13:18-25
   1. A request for prayer, 13:18-19
   2. Prayer for the Church, 13:20-21
   3. A request to be heard, 13:22-23
   4. Greetings and grace, 13:24-25

I

THE REVELATION OF GOD
IN HIS SON

1:1–2:18

A. CHRIST THE CLIMAX OF REVELATION, 1:1-3

THE STARTING POINT of the Epistle to the Hebrews reaches the core of Christian affirmation—God has spoken! A succession of inspired writers from both Old and New Testaments bear witness to the fact that God has raised up spokesmen to declare His truth amid the errors to which fallen man is prone. If sinful man is to find his way back to God, only God Himself can reveal the way.

Theologians and philosophers reason out the possibility and the probability of revelation: God is all-powerful; therefore He can reveal Himself to men; He is all-loving; therefore He might be expected to do so. The Bible claims to be such a revelation.

Yet the Epistle to the Hebrews does not begin with argument. It states a truth which its readers will presume to be a basic presupposition: God has spoken!

The early church was composed of converts who had recently come from Judaism. Christianity was not considered to be a new religion, but the fulfillment of the hopes and promises of the old. A Christian was one who believed that Jesus of Nazareth was the promised Messiah of Israel. This conviction produced a life guided by the principle of faith in Him and willingness to do His will.

These converts brought their Bibles with them—the Torah, or Old Testament as it is known to us. The early Hebrew Christians and the Gentiles who subsequently entered the church declared that God had truly spoken "to the fathers by the prophets" (1:1) of the Old Testament.

As Christians, however, they noted a difference between the Old Testament revelation and its fulfillment in Christ. The revelation in times past took place "at sundry times" and "in divers manners." From Moses to Malachi was a period of about one thousand years. Two millennia passed from Abraham to Christ. Israel had a varied history, including a seminomadic period, one of bondage in Egypt, one of tribal anarchy (the Judges), and a centralized monarchy (under David and Solomon). After the division of the kingdom we read of exile (in Assyria and Babylonia), after which a remnant returned to Jerusalem and its immediate environs. Throughout these "sundry times" we can trace a succession of prophetic spokesmen, men such as Moses, Joshua, Samuel, Nathan, Elijah, Amos, Isaiah, and Jeremiah. Some of them wrote books. Others had their ministries recorded in the historical books of the Old Testament. Their world included Ur of the Chaldees, Haran, Shechem, Jerusalem, Egypt, and Babylon—the entire area of the "Fertile Crescent." Days of apostasy and days of spiritual triumph saw God's messengers declaring His will to Israel. Moses in the wilderness, Elijah on Mount Carmel, and Ezekiel in Babylon were representative of the "sundry times" of Old Testament revelation.

As God is infinite in His being, so He has many means through which His revelation could be mediated. God spoke through the dreams of a Joseph and a Daniel. Moses and Abraham saw Him "face to face." By the River Chebar, Ezekiel received apocalyptic visions. Unnamed writers were led of the Spirit to take extracts from the chronicles of Israelite and Judean kings or older epic literature such as the Book of the Wars of the Lord, or the Book of Jasher (Num. 21:14; Josh. 10:13; II Sam. 1:18). Law, history, poetry, prophecy, wisdom literature, sacred song and psalm—the Old Testament contains a library of books covering a variety of themes and forms. Hebrews declares that God used "divers manners" in revealing Himself to the fathers.

Looking to the Old Testament as the preparatory revelation of God, the Christian sees the final revelation in Christ. In contrast to the "sundry times" of the Old Testament, the author of Hebrews speaks of God's final revelation as made "in these last days" (1:2). The "last days" are the days prophesied in Old Testament Scripture. Jewish teachers frequently mentioned "the age to come" as the Messianic Age, the time when history finds its culmination in the appearance of the long awaited Messiah. The Epistle to the Hebrews asserts that the Messianic Age has come, the Messiah has appeared. Jesus is God's last word, and beyond Him nothing need be sought.

Prophets faithfully declared the Word of God, but

Jesus was God incarnate. The Son is creator, revealer, and goal of the historical processes. He is the "heir of all things," because He is the Son of the Father to whom all things ultimately belong. The very kingdoms of this world are to become the kingdoms of our Lord and His Christ.

The Son is declared to be the "brightness" (1:3) of the glory of God. God's essential glory cannot be known to man. John writes, "No man hath seen God at any time." He hastens to add, however, "the only begotten son, which is in the bosom of the Father, he hath declared him" (John 1:18). Christ, the Son, is the visible outshining of God's glory. The invisible God can be seen and known in the Person of His Son. It was in the Person of the Son that God appeared to the patriarchs of Israel.

Mankind exhibits a constant desire to "see" God. The heathen bowing before his idol is deluded into thinking that his is a real "image" of God. The desire is right, but the manifestation of it is wrong. God desires to be "seen," but He is only visible in the Person of Jesus, "the express image of his person."

Creation, providence, and redemption are attributed to the Son. He both "made the worlds" (1:2) and "upholds all things by the word of his power" (1:3). Both creation and redemption are described in Scripture as the work of the triune God. Hebrews 11:3 states, "Through faith we understand that the worlds were framed by the word of God." Paul writes that Jesus "is the image of the invisible God, the firstborn of every creature: for by him were all things created, that are in heaven, and that are in earth, visible and invisible, . . . all things were created by him, and for him: and he is before all things, and by him all things consist" (Colossians 1:15-17).

The prophets had spoken of one who would Himself bear the iniquity of us all (Isa. 53:6). Hebrews states that this has been done, the Son having "by himself purged our sins" (1:3). This fact emphasizes the futility of man in his efforts to remove his own sins and of the Old Testament ordinances which had to be constantly repeated, bearing witness to their inability to "purge the conscience from dead works." Their value is not minimized. They were part of that Law, which was a pedagogue, leading men to see their need of Christ, the one Redeemer from sin.

The redemptive ministry of Christ formed a prelude to the glorification of the Son "on the right hand of the Majesty on high." Paul tells us that it was because Christ humbled Himself, becoming obedient unto death, even the death of the Cross, that the Father "highly exalted him" (Phil. 2:7-9). The preincarnate Christ had a glory with the Father "before the world was" (John 17:5). The crucified Messiah, however, has a new position with all power in Heaven and on earth committed unto Him (Matt. 28:18). This is reflected in the words of Psalm 110:1, "The Lord said unto my Lord, Sit thou on my right hand, until I make thine enemies thy footstool."

The Epistle to the Hebrews underscores the superiority of God's revelation in Christ to every other revelation, real or fancied. God has spoken in One who brought the worlds into being, became our suffering Saviour, and now is seated at the place of favor and authority, at the right hand of the Father. His message must be one which commands reverent respect and holy awe.

B. CHRIST'S SUPERIORITY OVER THE ANGELS, 1:4-14

1. *He is the Son,* 1:4-6

The superiority of God's revelation in Christ to that which had earlier been mediated by the prophets is re-enforced by the demonstration that Jesus is superior to all angelic beings in His position as the divine Son.

Jesus is declared to have a more excellent name than the angels (1:4). This is the name by which sinners may be saved (Acts 4:12) and to which every knee must bow (Phil. 2:10). The name is expressive of the Person Himself, His glory and attributes. Angels have a name identifying them as messengers, serving God and His children. The name of Jesus, on the other hand, identifies Him as the Saviour of the world and the anointed (i.e. "Christ") of the Father. When the name "Son" is applied to Jesus, He is designated as the beloved of the Father, and heir of all things.

The argument for the superiority of Christ to the angels finds support in the Scriptures of the Old Testament. The author of Hebrews looked to his Bible for evidence of the unique sonship of Jesus. He found it in Psalm 2:7, "Thou art my Son, this day have I begotten thee," and II Samuel 7:14, "I will be his father, and he shall be my son." Although angels are collectively called "sons of God" (Job 1:6), Christ alone bears the title "the Son." The Psalmist spoke of the day when God's Son was begotten, doubtless a reference to the incarnation, although it is applied elsewhere to the resurrection (Acts 13:33).

David wished to build a temple to the Lord in Jerusalem, but he was told that this project had to be de-

ferred. God said, however, that an "house" would be
built for David (II Sam. 7:11). This house, or dynasty,
would reign over Israel forever (II Sam. 7:16). Of
David's son, God said, "I will be to him a Father" (1:5;
II Sam. 7:14). In a general sense Solomon may be regarded as David's son who built the "house" or Temple,
but the author of Hebrews sees these words as a prophecy of David's "greater" son, Jesus of Nazareth who bears
the distinctive title, "Son of God."

Not only is Jesus designated as Son, but He also is
accorded worship, which angels are called upon to render but never receive. The quotation seems to be taken
from Psalm 97:7c, rendered in A.V., "Worship him, all
ye gods," but translated in the Greek Septuagint as
"Worship him all ye angels" (1:6). The Septuagint version of Deuteronomy 32:43 has a similar translation.
Israelite faith never accorded worship to angels. The
thrice holy God of Israel alone is worthy of the worship
of His people; all other beings were created by Him and
are subject to Him.

2. *His reign is eternal,* 1:7-14

A contrast is drawn between the nature of angels and
that of the Son. Psalm 104:4 is quoted in verse 7: "Who
maketh his angels spirits; and his ministers a flame of
fire." According to the laws of Hebrew parallelism the
"angels" and the "ministers" must be related terms. Angels are ministers, servants of God. Jesus, however, is
deity: "Thy throne, O God, is for ever and ever: a scepter of righteousness is the scepter of thy kingdom" (Ps.
45:6). The fact that the Messianic king was anointed
with the oil of gladness above his fellows (Ps. 45:7) is a

further reminder of his preeminence. This is no mere
creature. He has the supreme place in accord with His
divine Sonship.

In an extended quotation from Psalm 102:26-28 the
eternity of the Son is contrasted with the transient nature
of the earth and the heavens—"They shall perish; but
thou remainest" (1:11). To none but the Son has the
Father addressed the words, "Sit on my right hand, until
I make thine enemies thy footstool" (1:13; Ps. 110:1).
The Lord Jesus is seated "far above all principality, and
power, and might, and dominion, and every name that is
named, not only in this world, but also in that which is
to come" (Eph. 1:21).

By way of contrast to the exalted Son, we are reminded that angels are "ministering spirits" (1:14).
They are servants of God and His people. The Christian
is to be thankful for their ministry, as for every gift of
God's love. He recognizes Jesus, however, in a unique
position. As the Son of the Father, He alone receives the
absolute loyalty of the regenerate heart.

C. The Danger of Neglecting Salvation Through the Son, 2:1-4

The author of Hebrews has shown the claims of Christ
to the absolute loyalty of His people. God's last word is
Christ, the fulfillment of the prophetic hopes of Israel.
This Christ holds a unique relationship to the Father and
stands in contrast to angels, who are created beings and
servants of God and His people.

On this doctrinal basis, a warning is given. Men must
listen to the Son. It was necessary during the Old Testament economy to give heed to the word mediated

through angels. Paul stated that the Law "was ordained through angels by the hand of a mediator" (Gal. 3:19). This Law was steadfast, so that "every transgression and disobedience received a just recompence of reward" (2:2). When Nadab and Abihu offered "strange fire" before the Lord they died (Lev. 10:1-7). Achan took of the spoil of Jericho, and Israel was defeated on the field of battle until he and his family were stoned (Josh. 7). Although provision was made for the one who had sinned "through ignorance," the Israelite who sinned "with an high hand" died without mercy. God was not arbitrary, but a strict concept of justice was maintained.

The argument proceeds from the lesser to the greater. If judgment fell on those who transgressed the Law given through the mediation of angels, how much more serious will be the state of the one who rejects the Word of God's Son! We, now, should give even "more earnest heed" (2:1) than did those who lived under the former economy.

The warning contains an unanswerable question: "How shall we escape if we neglect so great salvation?" (2:3). Emphasis is properly placed on the "we." Those who perished under the Mosaic economy are a warning to us. The Gospel has brought greater privileges, and greater responsibilities. We dare not presume upon God's grace. His standard of righteousness has not altered, and He still expects obedience from His people.

This "great salvation" of the Messianic Age was first proclaimed by Jesus Himself. He both "proclaimed" the good tidings of salvation and made them possible by the sacrifice of Himself. This word did not cease with the death, resurrection, and ascension of the Messiah, however. He commissioned His disciples to proclaim the Gospel to every creature, assuring them of His continuing presence and of the power of the Holy Spirit.

The preaching of the Gospel was accompanied by "signs and wonders, and . . . divers miracles, and gifts of the Holy Ghost according to his own will" (2:4). These terms refer to the various types of miracles experienced in the early Church. "Signs" bore testimony to Christ as the Messiah. Jesus showed Himself Lord of nature by stilling the storm on Galilee. All who observed such acts were brought face to face with the claims of Christ. "Wonders" such as the feeding of the five thousand, and "miracles" of power, such as the casting out of demons, likewise served to authenticate the mission of Jesus. The risen Lord continued His ministry through the "gifts of the Holy Ghost" granted to the Church (I Cor. 12:1-11).

D. The Son and Humanity, 2:5-18

1. *Man's lowliness and dignity,* 2:5-8

As the contrast between Christ and the angels is continued, our attention is focused on the future. Not only was Christ operative in the creation of all things, including the angels, but He is ruler of the "age to come" (2: 5). Angels may be honored as God's creatures, but rule has been entrusted to the Son. Human history will not end in futility, but in the reign of Christ. His death has redeemed men, and it also brings about the removal of the curse on nature (Rom. 8:22-23).

The eighth Psalm asks the pointed question:

> What is man, that thou are mindful of him? Or the Son of Man that thou visitest him? (2:6)

The question arose from the Psalmist's contemplation of nature (Ps. 8:3). In contrast to the vastness of God's creation, man appears to be insignificant. Why should God care at all about man? Does He not have much else in which He may delight? The question is not answered. Instead we read:

> Thou madest him a little [or "for a little while"] lower than the angels,
> Thou crownedst him with glory and honor, . . .
> Thou hast put all things in subjection under his feet.
> (2:7-8)

The subject is still man. The expression "son of man" in Psalm 8 is synonymous with "man." Man was made as a creature of honor. He was given dominion over the earth (Gen. 1:28). Yet, "now we see not yet all things put under him" (2:8).

2. The necessity for the incarnation, 2:9-18

a. To fulfill God's gracious purpose, 2:9-10

Man was created as a noble creature, with capacity to glorify God and live a life of richness and honor. What happened? Why is it that he does not have the dominion assigned to him? The answer is an obvious one—sin. Man fell from his innocency and lives as a rebel. The original place of honor has been vacated.

Although we may be disappointed as we look upon man, Hebrews reminds us that we should look elsewhere. In Adam, man sinned. We do not see man in the place of dominion, but we can look to a man—the one perfect man, Jesus. Although essentially God, He "was made a little lower than the angels" (2:9), i.e. He became a man. The Word was made flesh and dwelt among us. The Son of God took upon Himself our humanity. As man, He suffered the death of the Cross. Now, however, the glorified Man, Christ Jesus, is "crowned with glory and honor" (2:9). Man sinned, but the Man, Christ Jesus, is the Redeemer from sin. Man disobeyed, but the Man, Christ Jesus, was "obedient unto death" (Phil. 2: 8).

Not only does Jesus, as man, exhibit in His Person the will of the Father, for mankind, but He is so identified with His people, those who commit their lives unto Him, that they become a new humanity. By the grace of God He tasted death for every man (2:9).

The words "tasted death" mean more than "died." Death is the natural lot of fallen man. "The wages of sin" cannot be refused by the members of sinful humanity. The death of Jesus, on the other hand, was very different. He who was without sin and therefore not under the curse of mortality "tasted" death in order that the sons of men who trust in Him might be spared that ordeal. "In his own body on the tree" He paid the debt for the sins of His people.

> There was no other good enough to pray the price
>   of sin;
> He only could unlock the gate of heaven and let
>   us in.

Now death is not a source of terror to the Christian. When Stephen was stoned he simply "fell asleep" (Acts 7:60) after seeing a vision of the risen Christ standing to welcome His faithful servant home.

It is with reverence we read that the "captain" of our

salvation was made perfect through sufferings (2:10).
Perfection of character, absolute holiness, was His before Calvary. Yet the word "perfect" has another sense.
It may speak of completeness. As the Redeemer, Jesus
had to redeem. He was the sinless teacher, but man
needed more than a teacher, however holy. The completion of the work for which Jesus entered the world demanded suffering. Jesus suffered and died in order to
bring "many sons unto glory."

Jesus is now "crowned with glory and honor" (2:9).
From the depths of humiliation He arose to the heights
of exaltation at the Father's right hand. He is now "in
glory." Yet Jesus does not enjoy this glory alone. He
endured the cross "for the joy that was set before him"
of bringing "many sons unto glory." He identified Himself with humanity in becoming "the son of man." Now
He associates us with Himself in giving us the "power
[or "authority"] to become the sons of God" (John 1:12).
He was "sanctified," or set apart, to enter the world as
Redeemer. His people are likewise sanctified, set apart
as those whose lives are now indwelt by His Spirit and
lived to His glory.

b. To make one the Saviour and the saved, 2:11-15

The union of the Redeemer with the redeemed is set
forth in bold terminology. The Sanctifier and the sanctified have a common origin—in God and His sovereign
will. He is not ashamed to call them "brethren" (2:11).
They are not only "sons of God," but also "joint-heirs
with Christ."

The words of David (Ps. 22:22) are quoted to illustrate the identification of Christ with His people:

I will declare thy name unto my brethren, in the
midst of the church will I sing praise unto thee
(2:12)

As the Psalmist had "brethren" among whom he praised
the Lord, so Jesus is associated with His "brethren,"
with whom the Father delights to have fellowship as they
are united by faith to His beloved Son.

Two other verses from the Old Testament, Isaiah 8:17
and Isaiah 8:18, are quoted as from the lips of Jesus
(2:13): "I will put my trust in Him" and "Behold I and
the children which God hath given me." The first is an
expression of personal faith in God. In the second, the
prophet Isaiah associated himself with his children,
given him by God as "signs" to the generation to which
he ministered. As Isaiah both trusted God, and stood
before God with his children, so Jesus is presented to us
in Scripture as wholly mindful of the Father's will, trust-
ing Him in every detail. He, too, does not stand alone,
but with His "children."

This identification began with the incarnation. The
children are "flesh and blood," i.e. human beings. To be
identified with them, He had to become a partaker of
"flesh and blood" (2:14). The real deity and the real
humanity are both stressed in Hebrews. Only as Jesus
became true man could He purchase our redemption.

Jesus became man in order that He might die. This
statement runs counter to our usual concept of God's
will. Life is a gift of God, but life sometimes comes
"through death." Satan is the prince of death. As man
obeyed his voice, sin entered the world, and death by sin.
Yet in Christ, death became the medium for the destruction of the power of Satan. The Devil himself is a de-

feated foe, defeated by the power of the Prince of Life.

The redemptive work of Christ delivers man from the "fear of death" (2:15). Sin is a dread reality. Man is conscious of his dependence upon God and of the fact that a day of reckoning is at hand. To the Christian, however, the sting of death is removed. Because of sin, man fears death, but Jesus has taken on Himself the sin of His people. If we reckon that the "wages of sin is death," we also glory that "the gift of God is eternal life through Jesus Christ our Lord." The fear of death is a "bondage," but the Christian is God's free man, freed from fear and enabled to draw nigh to the very throne of grace through Christ, "the new and living way," with the utmost confidence of acceptance. Paul could triumphantly declare, "To me to live is Christ, and to die is gain."

    c. To enable the Saviour to sympathize with the saved, 2:16-18

The glorious purposes of God in redemption are addressed to men, not to angels. Hebrews 2:16 in the Authorized Version appears at first sight to refer to the incarnation—"He took not on him the nature of angels." Able scholars, including Delitzsch and Westcott, consider the verse a continuation of the theme of redemption. Jesus did not, according to this understanding, take hold of angels to redeem them, but rather directed His atoning love toward the fallen human race. It was specifically to the "seed of Abraham" that His ministry was first directed. When "his own received him not," the message was sent to the "highways and hedges" where all—circumcised and uncircumcised, barbarian, Scythian, bond and free, were given the message of God's boundless love.

In order to redeem His "brethren" Jesus was "made like unto his brethren" (2:17). He became a true man. A High Priest must be a human being, chosen from among men. If he is to understand and represent fallen humanity before the Majesty on High, he must know the meaning of temptation and suffering. One of the early heresies in the Christian church was known as Docetism. The Docetists said that Jesus "seemed" to be a real man, but He was not really human. The humanity of Christ was an illusion. The author of Hebrews leaves no room for Docetism. To become our High Priest, Jesus had to share our humanity—even to the point of suffering.

The priesthood had both a Godward and a manward aspect. There was a ministry in "things pertaining to God" in order to effect "reconciliation for the sins of the people" (2:17). As the High Priest of the Old Testament presented sacrifices to God in order to effect reconciliation, so Jesus offered Himself to the Father. As High Priest, Jesus was "faithful." He performed the ministry entrusted to Him. He was also "merciful." He had compassion on His people. Although He was personally free from sin, the humanity of Jesus enabled Him to know the motives of men, their temptations, and their weaknesses. The bruised reed He did not break. Even the Jerusalem which rejected Him was the object of His tender love. He wept over its sins. He spared no invective in denouncing the sham pretense of the hypocritical Pharisee, but the penitent sinner found Him ever ready to offer a word of understanding and forgiveness.

II

THE FAITHFUL SAVIOUR

3:1—4:13

A. Christ, as Son, Superior to Moses, as Servant,
3:1-6

The ministries of Jesus and Moses have a number of things in common. Moses was the "mediator" of the covenant which God made with Israel at Mount Sinai. Through him, God brought His people from Egyptian bondage to the borders of the land of promise—the earthly inheritance of Israel, which may be contrasted with the "heavenly calling" of the Church of Jesus Christ (3:1).

Both Moses and Jesus are described as "faithful." They each had solemn responsibilities, committed to them directly by God. In each instance there was a rejection by a portion of the very people who would be benefited most by their ministries. When Moses' right to act as an arbiter in the affairs of his people was questioned, he escaped to the desert. Faithful to the call given at the burning bush, Moses returned to Egypt and became the leader of the exodus.

Similarly Jesus was "faithful." The Father declared

His pleasure in the Son, and Jesus Himself declared, "I do always those things that please him."

The fact of divine appointment is also evident both in the call and ministry of Moses and in that of Jesus. The providential protection of the infant Moses, his time spent with his own mother, his years of training as "the son of Pharaoh's daughter" all prepared him for the day when God called and commissioned Moses as His spokesman to Pharaoh and to Israel.

The "appointment" of Jesus is a solemn fact which defies analysis. Scripture makes it clear that He was the "Lamb slain from the foundation of the world" (Rev. 13: 8). God's purpose to redeem man through the sacrifice of Jesus antedates creation itself. The purpose of God was revealed at the time of the incarnation. Mary knew that her Son was to be the promised Messiah, and wise men sought the "king of the Jews." A public proclamation of the mission of Jesus took place at the time of His baptism. God's word, "Hear ye him," was an address to Israel giving the divine approval to the ministry of Jesus.

The fact of appointment by God and the attitude of faithfulness are characteristics which Jesus and Moses had in common. The author of Hebrews, however, wishes to underscore the differences between the mediator of the Old and the New Covenants. In each instance there is a relationship to the "house," i.e. the household of faith. Moses was a faithful servant (literally, domestic servant) in the household (3:5), whereas Jesus is the "builder" of the household (3:3). It is the household of God, with many servants. Christ is the Son and heir. All of the Father's property is His by right of inheritance. Thus Jesus and Moses stand on a significantly different footing.

Christ thus occupies the position of both builder and Son in the household of faith. Moses was a part of that household, and occupied the place of an honored servant. This is not stated to downgrade Moses but to teach the essential difference between Moses and Jesus. The ministry of Moses anticipated that of Jesus. Moses bore testimony to those things which were to be spoken later (3:5), namely the things which pertain to salvation. In Christ, these promises are fulfilled. We are His house (3:6). We have a ground for confidence and hope, which we are urged to maintain without wavering. The teaching concerning the superiority of Christ to Moses was designed to encourage any who might be tempted to waver to follow on in loving obedience and loyalty to Christ.

B. CONSEQUENCES OF ISRAEL'S UNBELIEF, 3:7-11

Although Moses was faithful to God, the generation of which he was a part perished in the wilderness. This fact served as a warning to the generation which heard the Gospel of Christ and was in danger of rejecting it.

The wilderness period is defined as the "provocation" (3:8). The people provoked God to anger. They were the recipients of His grace, but they were guilty of ingratitude, murmuring, and disobedience. Although they pledged themselves to keep His law, in fact they broke it.

The unbelief of Israel in the wilderness resulted in the loss of an entire generation. Those who left Egypt, except for Caleb and Joshua, died in the wilderness. They hoped to reach the Promised Land, but they never did. In wrath God swore, "They shall not enter into my rest" (3:11).

C. Warning Against Unbelief, 3:12-19

The hardness of heart on the part of the generation which perished in the wilderness is here compared with the hardness of heart of those who rejected the word of Christ. The message is given in the form of a warning: "Take heed . . . lest there be in any of you an evil heart of unbelief" (3:12). The logic is clear. If unbelief prevented the generation in the wilderness from entering God's rest, it will also prevent men in the writer's generation from entering the "rest" God has for His people.

Great stress is placed on the word "today" (3:7, 13). The author of Hebrews is aware that he is living in momentous times. It is not enough simply to be concerned with past history or with prospects for the future. There is the all-important "today," when God is speaking decisively to His people. The importance of serving one's own generation, living boldly for God at the present moment, is a challenge which finds ample justification in Scripture. Now is the acceptable time! We have no promise of a tomorrow. The claims of Christ must be weighed and acted upon without delay.

In the light of the momentous issues actually matters of life and death, it is well that we be aware of the "deceitfulness of sin" (3:13). Satan comes in the form of an angel of light. His suggestion that we partake of the forbidden fruit is always couched in language which suggests that we will be better and happier for the experience. Actually he is the father of lies, the master of deceit. The lust of the flesh, the lust of the eye, and the pride of life will lead us in one direction, but the "life more abundant" in Christ is based on higher and holier considerations.

Three serious questions are posed for the diligent reader. These serve as a review of the lesson under discussion. The first concerns those who "when they had heard, did provoke" (3:16). The answer is obvious: "Did not all they that came out of Egypt by Moses?" A second question asks, "With whom was he displeased forty years?" The answer is written on the pages of Old Testament history, "Was it not with them that sinned, whose bodies fell in the wilderness?" The third question reaches the climax, "To whom sware he that they should not enter into his rest?" The answer is simple and pertinent, "Them that were disobedient [believed not]."

The unbelief of Israel is specifically recorded in Numbers 12. Spies had been sent to the promised land to determine the feasibility of pressing into Canaan. The majority of the spies agreed that the land was good, but insisted that the forces of Israel could not hope to battle the gigantic Canaanites. They likened themselves to "grasshoppers" in contrast to the tall "sons of Anak." The assurance of Caleb and Joshua that God could be trusted to give victory to His people fell on deaf ears. The people turned back, the pilgrims becoming wanderers; the travelers, tramps. "So we see," the author of Hebrews says, "that they could not enter in because of unbelief" (3:19). Unbelief keeps the lost from sharing the blessing of salvation. It also keeps the Christian from sharing the fulness of God's blessing.

D. Exhortation to Faithfulness, 4:1-13

1. *A rest remains for the people of God*, 4:1-11

By way of personal application we read, "Let us therefore fear, lest, a promise being left us of entering into his rest, any of you should seem to come short of it" (4:1). If the generation that perished in the wilderness did not enter Canaan, what ground do we have for believing we shall enter the "rest" God has for His people? It is clear that disobedience on our part will have the same results which their disobedience produced (4:1, 11). A unity in God's dealings with His people in differing ages may be noted. He always demands faith, and unbelief consistently results in His judgments.

The appeal to history is clear. Unbelieving Israel did not enter rest (4:3, 5). Psalm 95:11 is quoted: "As I sware in my wrath, they shall not enter into my rest." Although "rest" in Canaan was the desire of Israel during the days of Moses and Joshua, a more basic need was (and is) the spiritual rest which is entered by faith. Only believers may enter this "true" rest. The Epistle to the Hebrews argues that Joshua ("Jesus" A.V.) did not bring Israel into the true rest, for Psalm 95:11, written much later than Joshua, spoke of rest as yet future.

The conclusion of the author is clear, "There remaineth . . . a sabbath rest for the people of God" (4:9). God Himself had rested on the sabbath day (4:4). This marked the completion of His "works." Man, too, has been assigned his work, and may anticipate a future rest. This was not achieved under Joshua, but through Jesus such a spiritual rest may be entered, for "he that is entered into his rest hath himself also rested from his works, as God did from his" (4:10). This is not a temporary expedient but the perfect sabbath rest of God.

An exhortation in the form of a paradox follows this instruction: "Let us labor therefore to enter into that rest" (4:11). The warning that some of Joshua's generation failed is a reminder that we, too, may fail. Yet the very purpose of the epistle is to prevent us from failing. The "gospel" to Moses' generation was the hope of entering Canaan (4:2). Since it was not received in faith, they perished in the wilderness. We, too, have a "Gospel," but ours deals with the "rest" which even Joshua did not provide—the rest in Christ. Those who by faith come to Him find the gift of rest. This "sabbath rest" does not mean the end of service to God and works which are the fruit of the Spirit. On the contrary, this rest makes such works possible. It is not simply the rest of Heaven but the rest of the spirit in Christ, which is a kind of earnest of Heaven.

2. *The omniscient God is judge,* 4:12-13

Instrumental in bringing men into the "rest" of which the Epistle to the Hebrews speaks is the "Word of God." We began with the statement that God had spoken through prophets and, finally, in His Son. Here we are reminded of the nature of God's Word. It is "living, and active" ("quick and powerful"). As such it is meaningful to us, applicable to our lives. The Bible contains many facts, but it is not to be treated like an encyclopedia. It acts upon the soul of man so that he can never be quite the same again. The Word is described as "sharper than any twoedged sword." It pierces men to the quick, laying bare their most secret intentions and motives. The Word "discerns the thoughts and intents of the heart."

It may be a disturbing thought, but it should bring comfort to know that "all things are naked and opened unto the eyes of him with whom we have to do" (4:13). This can be said of none but God. Our dearest friends and the members of our families know us only in part. The very proneness of our hearts to forget God is known by Him. He knows our frame, remembers that we are dust. It is with this assurance that we can wholly entrust ourselves to Him. We can only enter into His rest as we trust Him completely. His Word, which bears testimony to His Person, will help us to do that.

III

THE GREAT HIGH PRIEST

4:14—10:18

A. Confidence in Christ's Priesthood, 4:14-16

BASIC TO JUDAISM before the destruction of Jerusalem (A.D. 70) was the priest who officiated in the Jerusalem Temple. There, on set occasions, animals were slain as sacrifices and prayers were made to God on behalf of the sinful Israelite. Such concepts had existed in Israel from earliest times. The Bible records sacrifices made by Abel and his brother Cain. Noah offered sacrifice after the flood, and the patriarchs, Abraham, Isaac, and Jacob, regularly built altars and offered sacrifices.

At Mount Sinai the Jewish sacrificial system was regularized. A specific structure, the Tabernacle, later replaced by the Temple, was set apart for the priestly ministry. Aaron and his sons were consecrated as priests, and a system of offerings and holy days was incorporated into the life of Israel.

The Christian church is built on Old Testament foundations. The Law was not abolished, but fulfilled in Christ. Hebrews declares (4:14): ". . . we have a great

High Priest." Our High Priest, Jesus, has "passed through the heavens," and is now enthroned at the Father's right hand. His exalted position is the ground of Christian confidence. The earthly High Priest could enter the Holy of Holies but once a year. Our High Priest is now in Heaven where He is seated at the Father's right hand.

Our exalted High Priest is in no sense remote from us, however. This is asserted in the form of a double negative: "we have not an High Priest which cannot be touched with the feeling of our infirmities" (4:15). Our High Priest knows the nature of humanity in that He Himself became a man. One characteristic of man, in his present state, is temptation. Jesus was tempted as true man. The entire range of human temptations, the lust of the flesh, the lust of the eye, and the pride of life, was experienced by the Saviour. Yet He differed from the rest of mankind in that He was "without sin." Thus Christ takes us back to the period before Adam's fall. In Adam all die, but in Christ all are made alive.

Christ is perfectly able and perfectly willing to intercede for us. Assured of His love, we may approach Him with confidence. This is one of the characteristics of the New Covenant. The ancient Israelite had to stand afar off, unable to enter the "Holy Place," much less the "Holy of Holies," the throne room of God. With Christ, our High Priest, in Heaven itself, the believer need not stand in the distance, or timidly seek intermediaries through whom God may be approached. He now has confidence —a holy "boldness," for Jesus has identified Himself with us and enabled us to enter the very presence of God.

B. CHRIST'S POSSESSION OF THE ESSENTIAL QUALITIES FOR PRIESTHOOD, 5:1-10

1. *Sympathy with men,* 5:1-3

Both the Levitical priesthood and Christ, our great High Priest, meet certain qualifications or prerequisites. The "order" of Christ's priesthood differs from that of the Levitical priests, but both were chosen from among men and accepted by God. Stress has already been placed on the true humanity of Jesus. He was chosen from among those whom He was to represent before God. Man brought sin into the world, and it was necessary that deliverance should come by man.

As priest, Jesus was "ordained for men" (5:1), or appointed to act on behalf of men in relation to God. Priestly and prophetic ministries may be contrasted. The prophet, as the spokesman for God, addresses man whereas the priest approaches God with his prayer and his offering on behalf of men. Both of these ministries were undertaken by Christ.

The offerings of Jesus, like those of the Old Testament priests, are described as "gifts and sacrifices for sins." The first term speaks of all offerings, whether bloodless or bloody. In the Levitical rites provision was made for a meal offering as well as the sacrifice of "bulls and goats." The term for "sacrifice," however, implies the shedding of the blood of the victim. Theologians frequently speak of the "active obedience" and the "passive obedience" of Christ. The terms may not be entirely satisfactory, but the distinction is valid. Christ obeyed the Father perfectly in His life ("active obedience"), but the moment for which the Word became flesh was the sacrifice at Calvary when He "became obedient unto death." The words and the works of the Son of God form a necessary prelude to His offering of Himself for the sins of His people. A priest must have a sacrifice, and Jesus offered Himself as an atonement for sin.

The ministry of the priest is one of "compassion" (5:2). The sympathy is itself a form of suffering. The priest does not side with the sinner against the righteous demands of the holy God, but he does show a sympathy with the sinner at the very time he expresses, by word and act, severity toward sin. Compassion is expressed toward the "ignorant," them that are out of the way"— the wayward. The Levitical offerings made provision for the one who sinned "in ignorance" (Num. 15:27-31), but the one who sinned "presumptuously" was accorded no mercy. The latter sins involved a willful renunciation of the lordship of the God of Israel. Although all sin is hateful in the sight of God, a distinction is made between the one who sins because of the infirmities of the flesh and the insolent rebel. The former has proper motives, and may experience the hand of God in discipline to bring him to the place of obedience to God's will. The latter meets judgment, as did Dathan and Abiram or Korah and his company. In such cases it was not left to man to make judgments; God Himself administered His own penalties. Even such wicked deeds as the murder of Uriah by adulterous David were forgiven. David was clearly "out of the way" when he committed these sins, and he was punished for them, but restoration to divine favor was possible after his repentance.

The human priest "himself also is compassed with infirmity" (5:2). He has experienced human weakness and frailty. All of the sinless infirmities of the human race were shared by Jesus. He experienced the pangs of hunger at the very beginning of His ministry and uttered the cry, "I thirst," at its close. He craved the friendship and loyalty of His disciples, but they all forsook Him and fled. Peter, James, and John would not watch with Him "one hour" in the garden, and Judas, one of the twelve, betrayed Him for thirty pieces of silver. He did mighty works in Capernaum, but it rejected Him as did Nazareth, the city of His youth. He experienced poverty from the moment of His birth in a stable in Bethlehem to His burial in Joseph's tomb. It was said of Him that "the Son of man hath not where to lay his head."

In contrast to Christ, the Levitical priesthood not only experienced the infirmities which grow out of our humanity but those which are associated with sin. Because of this fact, the Levitical priest must make sacrifices "as for the people, so also for himself" (5:3). He has been tempted, and he has yielded to temptation. There is an implication here that the Levitical priest cannot serve as an effectual mediator. He has personal guilt which requires atonement. For this reason help must come from another.

2. *God's appointment*, 5:4-10

The call of any priest must be divine in origin. Aaron was called of God, and his descendants served because of their place in the divine economy. When King Saul attempted to offer sacrifice, a ministry reserved for the priests, he was reprimanded by Samuel and told of God's judgment which would fall on his "house" or family. Failure to be a member of the line chosen by God to officiate as the priests was itself evidence that another vocation must be chosen. Men had no right to become priests by personal choice. It was a ministry directed toward God, and one who undertook it apart from God's choice was guilty of presumption.

Jesus, however, although not of the line of Aaron, was clearly called of God to His priestly work. Two portions of Old Testament Scripture are cited in proof of this. Psalm 2:7 tells that the Father chose Christ: "Thou art my Son; this day have I begotten thee." Both at the baptism of Jesus and at the moment of His transfiguration the Father designated Jesus as the Son who was to be heard and obeyed.

More specific, however, is the reference to Christ's priesthood in Psalm 110:4, "Thou art a priest for ever after the order of Melchizedek." This provides the key to the contention that the priesthood of Christ is superior to that of Aaron and his descendants. Although all priests in Israel had to be of the Aaronic line, the Law itself spoke of a pre-Aaronic priest who was recognized by no less a personage than Abraham. Melchizedek had been the priest-king of the city-state of Jerusalem (Salem) at the time Abraham had rescued Lot from his captors. Subsequently the Psalmist spoke of an ideal and everlasting priestly line after the order of Melchizedek.

As the chosen priest, Jesus fulfilled an important prerequisite to His work as mediator of His people. The author of Hebrews next gives us a challenging picture of the human Jesus struggling in prayer. We see the Saviour offering "prayers and supplications" (5:7), expressive of a heart burdened at the prospect of impending calamity.

We immediately think of the agony of Gethsemane, although the Gospels make it clear that Jesus often spent prolonged seasons in prayer. Specifically we read that He prayed "unto him that was able to save him from death" (5:7). Does this mean that Jesus sought to avoid death? Delitzsch suggests that the words which may be literally rendered "to save *out of* death" refer to a salvation from spiritual death. According to this view, Jesus shrank from the spiritual consequences of His death, experiencing the wrath of God on behalf of the sinners for whom He died. The answer came in the strength which the Father gave the Son to bear the sin of the world.

Although it might seem that the prayer of Jesus was not answered, for Jesus died, it is clear that a glorious answer was forthcoming. Jesus overcame the power of death. Jesus tasted death, but in so doing He opened the vistas of endless life for His people. The temptation of Jesus "in all points" included the issues of death, but He accepted the Father's will and "for the joy . . . set before him" endured its agonies.

God's answer came to Jesus "in that he feared" (5: 7). We are faced with the submissive and obedient Man, Christ Jesus. The Saviour stood in reverential awe before the revelation of the Father's will. Fear in this sense is not an attitude of apprehension or dread. It is a positive virtue, the response of the individual who properly perceives the nature of God and the demands He makes upon His creatures. Although God incarnate, the Son wholly submitted to the will of the Father, accepted it as good, and acted upon it.

Discipline is a mark of sonship. The deity of Jesus

might seem to have removed Him from the necessity of obedience and suffering, but such was not the case. Jesus did not call legions of angels to deliver Him from His enemies, a royal prerogative which He might have used. Jesus was not only willing to obey; He obeyed. This did not render His sinlessness greater, but it did "perfect" or complete His preparation for death on the Cross as the divine Redeemer.

The result of the successful accomplishment of the high-priestly mission of Jesus is briefly summarized: "eternal salvation unto all them that obey him" (5:9). Jesus was obedient to the Father. Now He seeks the obedience of faith of all who would share His blessings. Faith may be regarded as the response of obedience to the preaching of the message of redemption in Christ. The salvation enjoyed is "eternal," both timeless in quality and perfect in character. It speaks of the riches of God's grace toward the people He would honor.

C. Spiritual Dullness of the Hebrews, 5:11—6:12

1. *Lack of growth in knowledge, 5:11-14*

The writer of the Epistle to the Hebrews is enthused with his subject, but he becomes disturbed because of the spiritual immaturity of his audience. Jesus was "called of God an high priest after the order of Melchizedek" (5:10), a truth filled with meaning to be expounded in chapter 7. Much is to be said of Melchizedek, but the Christians are "dull of hearing" (5:11), immature and hence not prepared to receive spiritual instruction.

Immature Christians not only hurt themselves, by robbing themselves of the spiritual benefits which accompany maturity, but they rob others also. Christians should be "teachers" (5:12), sharing their spiritual blessings with others, both within and without the Church. It is the entire Church that has been called to a teaching ministry, although some individuals have special gifts (Eph. 4:11-12). The Great Commission includes the command, "teach all nations" (Matt. 28:19).

Instead of being teachers, however, the immature Christians had need that one teach them again "the first principles of the oracles of God" (5:12). Teachers who should be reaching the lost must spend their time re-instructing the immature. The word rendered "first principles" is used in Greek to designate the alphabet. You need to be taught your ABC's all over again! This instruction is in the "oracles of God." The term reflects the high concept of Biblical inspiration taught in Hebrews. Here it underscores the sinfulness of neglect. You have let slip from you the elementary truths of Scripture—God's Word! If this is so, then, truly, you must be taught again. These lessons are all-important. But, the impassioned plea continues, you should move from the "milk" stage of spiritual life to the "meat" stage.

The illustration is, of course, drawn from physical life. We rejoice when a child is born into the world. Great care is taken to meet his every need. Milk is quite sufficient in the earliest days of his life. Life does not remain stationary, however. Physical growth demands a varied diet. The analogy to spiritual truth is evident. We are commanded to "grow in grace, and in the knowledge of our Lord and Saviour Jesus Christ" (II Pet. 3:18).

The ideal is expressed in Ephesians 4:15 as a growing up "into him in all things." Paul says, "When I became a man, I put away childish things" (I Cor. 13:11). He further exhorted the Corinthians, "Brethren, be not children in understanding: howbeit in malice be ye children, but in understanding be men" (I Cor. 14:20).

The milk drinker, we read, "is unskilful in the word of righteousness" (5:13). There is no hint, of course, that we should not cherish the "milk"—the rudiments of Christian faith. The facts of God's grace in Christ should always be precious to the believer—

> I love to tell the story
> For those who know it best
> Are hungering and thirsting
> To hear it like the rest.

This need not be *taught* to the believer constantly, however. He should rest in the great truth of God's love and the redemption wrought by Christ at Calvary, and move on to a life of service.

The "strong meat" Christian is mature (5:14). He is described as one who uses the facilities which God has placed at his disposal. He is not simply a witness to the battles of life. The worldling may be a disinterested spectator in the battle between truth and error, but the Christian must be an active participant. The Hebrews were rooting for the side of truth, but they had not joined the battle for truth. Babies are excused from fighting, but meat-eaters should be where the going is rough. The Christian is called upon to put on his armor (Eph. 6:11) and enter the fray.

The distinction between good and evil (5:14) involves more than the theoretical. It is "by reason of use" that the senses are "exercised to discern both good and evil."

Since the "milk Christian" is unable to enter the battle, he is forced to act like a child, "tossed to and fro, and carried about with every wind of doctrine, by the sleight of men, and cunning craftiness, whereby they lie in wait to deceive" (Eph. 4:14). As the Christian moves into the arena he is enabled to identify the false and reject it in favor of the true. He is not, of course, infallible, and may make many errors of judgment in the process of "growing," but his powers of discernment mature even as he matures.

2. Need for pressing on to maturity, 6:1-3

In his appeal for spiritual maturity, the author of Hebrews bids us leave "the principles of the doctrine of Christ" (6:1). The "leaving" means advancement. There is no hint that we should forsake or neglect the basic doctrines of which he has been speaking. Milk is necessary, and there is a time in life when we live on it. The appeal, however, is to maturity. Move on from the ABC's unto maturity ("perfection").

We are not to lay again "the foundation of repentance from dead works" (6:1). Repentance toward God and faith in Jesus Christ are Christian fundamentals. The Christian has seen himself as a sinner who has broken the Law of God. He has seen sin as an offence to the God who loved him and sent His Son as the divine Redeemer. The very goodness of God leads to repentance (Rom. 2:4). This repentance involves a turning away from "dead works," i.e. works which are not the fruit of the Spirit of the living Christ. The works of the unbeliever are "dead" as well as evil. "Good works" are the fruit of salvation (Eph. 2:10). We have repented of our dead works as we have become children of life. We need not, however, go over all of that ground again. The foundation is there, but we must move on to maturity.

"Faith toward God" (6:1) is, of course, basic to the Christian experience. The one who comes to God must believe that "he is, and that he is a rewarder of them that diligently seek him" (Heb. 11:6). Here again we are reminded that we must build on Biblical fundamentals. This truth every Christian recognizes. From basic truths he can move on.

Among the basics of Christian doctrine from which the Christian must advance is "the doctrine of baptisms" (6:2). Although the Christian church knows but one baptism (Eph. 4:5), the Old Testament prescribed numerous "washings" or ceremonial lustrations which typified the cleansing which was required before any man could approach God. It was a fundamental of Christian faith to distinguish between the Christian rite of baptism, which accompanied a profession of faith in Christ, and the many ceremonial washings which were the mark of the pious Jew.

The "laying on of hands" was another element of Christian usage which the believer was expected to understand. The rite symbolized transfer. On the Day of Atonement hands were placed on the head of a goat as the priest confessed the sins of Israel (Lev. 16:21). Then the goat was sent away into the wilderness where he typically carried the sins which he bore, never to return with them again. Conversely, the laying on of the hands of Jesus brought healing to the sick (Mark 5:23). On the occasion of the consecration of the first deacons (Acts 6:6), the apostles "when they had prayed, . . . laid their hands on them." In all probability at the time of baptism, "hands" were laid upon the new Christians, symbolizing enduement with the Holy Spirit.

The Book of the Acts makes it clear that "resurrection from the dead" was an important element in the preaching of the early Church. The resurrection of Jesus had apologetic value. The Messiah of Israel had been crucified by wicked men, but God had raised Him up, and the disciples declared themselves witnesses to these things! Their confidence in the resurrection of Jesus gave them confidence that all who had "fallen asleep in Christ" (I Cor. 15:18) would also be raised from the dead.

"Eternal judgment" (6:2) was an important part of the message of the apostles. Jesus was declared to be "Judge of quick and dead" (Acts 10:42).

The Christians who received the Epistle to the Hebrews knew all of these doctrines. The author implies that he does not wish to spend time on them because they are basic fundamentals. He wishes to leave these principles—"if God permit" (6:3).

3. *Danger of falling away from Christ*, 6:4-8

One very practical reason for "going on" is the fact that a constant preoccupation with fundamentals will not convince the unconvinced anyway. Are there some who were "once enlightened" (6:4) and who are now struggling to see the light? The writer wishes to hold before such the uniqueness of the Gospel of Christ. Are there people who have been confronted with the message of eternal life and who have rejected it? If so, the argument continues, there is no other way of repentance and faith. One who comes by another way is a "thief and robber" (John 10:8).

Many believers have been troubled over these verses which seem to teach that a believer may finally lose his salvation. Words such as "enlightened," "tasted the heavenly gift," "made partakers of the Holy Ghost" (6:4), "tasted the good word of God, and the powers of the world to come" (6:5) seem, at first glance, at least, to describe true believers. It is true, of course, that many nominal Christians know something of the power of the Gospel. Judas Iscariot, although a "son of perdition," was one of the twelve apostles. Many Bible teachers, including Kenneth S. Wuest and Gleason L. Archer, hold that the people described in Hebrews 6:4-6 were not Christians at all, but individuals who had known the Gospel through a secondhand experience. William R. Newell observed that "tasting is not drinking," and R. A. Torrey spoke of a "quickening short of regeneration." The old Puritan divine, John Owen, said, "The persons here intended are not true and sincere believers."

B. F. Westcott in his commentary on Hebrews interprets the "impossible" as meaning "impossible for man." He implies that God can work effectively in such an individual, but there is no human hope for the individual who has tasted of God's grace and then turned back from Christ. W. H. Griffith Thomas suggests a modification of this. He says, "Active hostility to Christ, ever persisted in, cannot be a matter of restoration, though, of course, if the cause ceases to operate, the effect will cease to follow." In this sense, the term "impossible" is not taken in an absolute sense.

A popular viewpoint, held by Delitzsch and Lenski, is

that the sin of Hebrews 6 is identical with the sin against the Holy Spirit (Luke 12:8-10; Matt. 12:31; Mark 3:29). The men described would be guilty of the sin of imputing the work of the Spirit of God to Satan. They would be regarded as hardened sinners. There is, however, no hint that those who sinned against the Holy Spirit ever professed to be believers.

Others suggest that a hypothetical situation is presented in Hebrews 6. If a believer could so sin, the results would be as indicated. Such is not possible for a true believer, and the writer said: ". . . we are persuaded better things of you" (6:9).

The British writer, G. H. Lang, has given yet another viewpoint. He points to the analogy between the Israelites who perished in the wilderness and the Christians who turned their back upon Christ. The Israelites did not perish in the sense of going to Hell. They died. In the early Church, Ananias and Sapphira suffered physical death as a result of sin. Lang suggests that we are here dealing with true believers who meet God in judgment, but that the judgment is temporal rather than eternal. They have sinned unto death, but the death is physical, not spiritual.

It may be difficult to agree on the meaning of the passage, but certain things can be said with confidence. There is no hint here that anyone can have an "on again, off again" experience of salvation. If a saved person loses his salvation, it is forever! The many affirmations that a believer has eternal life and shall never perish cannot, however, be lightly set aside. The Spirit of God has here given us a solemn warning of severe judgments which will fall on anyone who turns his back upon the

Gospel of Jesus Christ. The very presence of this Scripture is a means used of the Spirit to prevent men from committing this sin.

Those who turn their backs upon the Lord are likened to the earth which drinks in the rain from heaven but yields thorns and briars (6:7-8). The thorns and briars are worthless, and so they are destroyed. Other earth, however, receiving rain, brings forth useful herbs and is blessed.

4. *Hope for better things,* 6:9-12

Although conscious of temptations among the Hebrew Christians, the author of the letter expresses his confidence in them: "Beloved, we are persuaded better things of you, and things that accompany salvation" (6: 9). The harsh words which he had just used were not to be interpreted as a lack of confidence. They serve as a warning and must not be lightly dismissed. Their purpose was to arouse the readers to the urgency of the situation and encourage them to follow on to Christian maturity.

The ground of confidence is the past life of the Hebrew Christians. Not only the writer, but "God is not unrighteous to forget your work and labor of love" (6:10). These people had ministered to the needy brethren in the name of Christ, and that ministry was continuing in spite of persecution and temptation. This good start should be continued (6:11). The earnestness of the believers in helping one another when in need should be continued in a further growth in grace. It is only through faith and patience (6:12) that the believer inherits the promises of God. There are temptations to be slothful

or lazy when the going is rough and the goal remote.
Nevertheless there has been a succession of faithful ones
(cf. Heb. 11), and we know that our efforts are not in
vain.

D. GOD'S WORD AND OATH, A GROUND OF CONFIDENCE, 6:13-20

An example of firmness in the midst of trials is the
patriarch Abraham (6:13). Men, when they wish to
solemnly avow a statement, call upon God as their witness by means of an oath. God, however, could swear
by none higher than Himself. God, by His own name,
swore to bless Abraham and multiply his descendants
(6:14). It was a long time before Abraham fathered the
child of promise, and there were times when Abraham
feared that God's word would not be fulfilled, but he
"patiently endured" (6:15) and, in his old age, looked
upon the face of Isaac.

In human relationships, men swear by one greater
than themselves. An oath taken by a man of integrity is
considered to be solemnly binding (6:16). If men trust
one another on the basis of an oath, how much more can
God be trusted when He takes an oath (6:17)? The
oath was taken not because God needed to reinforce
His word but to strengthen the faith of Abraham. It
was a mark of God's condescension. He wants to be
trusted, and gives His children every incentive to trust
in Him.

Abraham and all who are his children by faith can
trust God on the basis of "two immutable things" (6:18)
—God's Word, and God's oath. God's promise cannot be
broken, for it is the Word of the living God. God's oath

is trustworthy, for He has staked His divine reputation upon it. God cannot lie. Those who look to God in a world of trial may be tempted to be fearful. Can God care for me? Will He be true to His Word? We "who have fled for refuge to lay hold upon the hope set before us" have a "strong consolation" in God's Word and oath (6:18).

This hope has become an "anchor of the soul" (6:19). As such it will guarantee our safety, for it reaches from this world into glory. The presence of God is described in terms of the earthly Tabernacle where God sat enthroned between the cherubim in the Holy of Holies "within the veil." This was but a faint reflection of the true abode of God, Heaven itself. There God is, and there too is our anchor, "within the veil" in His very presence.

Not only is our anchor there, but our Forerunner is there, too. The resurrected Jesus is enthroned in the glory as the "firstfruits" of His redeemed people. In the heavenly Tabernacle, Jesus is performing His priestly ministry—"an high priest for ever after the order of Melchizedek" (6:20; Psalm 110:4).

E. CHRIST, A PRIEST AFTER THE ORDER OF MELCHIZEDEK, 7:1-28

1. *The history of Melchizedek, 7:1-3*

Melchizedek appears in the Book of Genesis as a character of ancient Biblical history. Abraham's nephew, Lot, had moved into the wicked city of Sodom and had become involved in its political life. When a coalition of kings from the East had defeated Sodom and its allies, Lot, along with other citizens of Sodom, was taken captive. Abraham, however, feeling a sense of responsibility for his nephew, gathered together the armed members of his household and journeyed to the far north of the country, where he surprised the enemy and rescued Lot and the other men of Sodom.

While returning from this successful campaign, Abraham stopped at Salem, usually identified with the place later known as Jerusalem, where he paid tithes to the priest-king of the city. Melchizedek blessed Abraham with the words, "Blessed be Abram of the most high God, possessor of heaven and earth; and blessed be the most high God, which hath delivered thine enemies into thy hand" (Gen. 14:19-20).

Who was this Melchizedek? The reference to him in Genesis 14 is the only mention of Melchizedek in the Old Testament historical books. He is pictured as the ruler of Salem. The city-states of the ancient Near East were frequently ruled by men who bore the title "king." Although the Israelites maintained a distinction between king and priest, the king being of the line of Judah through David and the priest of the line of Levi through Aaron, the two offices were usually combined among Israel's neighbors. Ancient Sumerian cities were ruled by *ensis*, priests who ruled as the reputed representatives of the gods. The Egyptian Pharaohs were actually given the honors of a deity.

Melchizedek is said to have been a priest of *El Elyon*, "the most high God." Abraham recognized Melchizedek as a true priest, considering *El Elyon* to be one of the names of the God whom he worshiped. We learn from this that even in the idolatrous times of Abraham there were those who worshiped the true God even though they were not members of the patriarch's family.

The meaning of the name and the office of Melchizedek is used in Hebrews to show that this ancient priest-king was a suitable type of Christ. Melchizedek is a compound name. The Hebrew word *melech* means "king," and *zedek* is the usual word for "righteousness." The compound form means "king of righteousness."

Melchizedek was also *melech* ("king") of Salem, a name related in meaning to the common Hebrew word *shalom* (Arabic, *salam*), "peace." The man who blessed Abraham thus had a double royalty—king of righteousness and king of peace. This is presented in Scripture as an ideal relationship: "Righteousness and peace have kissed each other" (Ps. 85:10). It is expressive of the person and ministry of Jesus, who is "full of grace and truth" (John 1:14). The Gospel declares that God is "just, and the justifier of him which believeth in Jesus" (Rom. 3:26).

Righteouness is an attribute of God. Righteousness is wholly lacking, however, in fallen, sinful man. How can man, then, live a life of righteousness in conformity to the sovereign demands of God? The distinctive Christian answer is, in the first instance, negative. Man cannot, of himself, ever hope to live a righteous life. This fact might lead to despair were it not for a companion fact—God, in sovereign grace, has made ample provision for man's need although man cannot provide for himself a righteousness:

> Therefore by the deeds of the law there shall no flesh be justified in his sight: for by the law is the knowledge of sin. But now the righteousness of God

> without the law is manifested, being witnessed by
> the law and the prophets; even the righteousness of
> God which is by faith of Jesus Christ unto all and
> upon all them that believe. (Rom. 3:20-22)

The Gospel proclaims that God has done for man that which man could not do for himself. God demands righteousness, but God has provided it in the Person of His Son. Righteousness is, then, imputed (Rom. 4:6) to the believer. Just as Christ, on Calvary, took our sins and in doing so was treated as a sinner, suffering the death of the Cross, so He has imputed His righteousness unto all believers so that they may be reckoned as righteous. It is because of this relationship to Christ, Who took our sins and gave to us His righteousness, that the believer now has access to the throne of grace.

Melchizedek was also king of peace. One of the names of the promised Messiah was, "Prince of Peace" (Isa. 9: 6). "Peace, good will toward men" (Luke 2:14) was part of the song of the angels in heralding the birth of "Christ the Lord." This peace is presented in the Epistle to the Romans as the result of the death and resurrection of Jesus:

> Who was delivered for our offences, and was raised
> again for our justification. Therefore being justified
> by faith, we have peace with God through our Lord
> Jesus Christ. (Rom. 4:25–5:1)

Peace marks the end of hostilities. In Scripture, *shalom* speaks of well-being. The sinner has no harmony within himself, in his relations to his fellow man, or in his relations with God. This harmony God Himself restores. The death of Christ made atonement for sin, and now

God through His "ambassadors" bids fallen men, "Be ye reconciled to God" (II Cor. 5:20). Christ restores the relationship between man and God which sin has broken. Although the results of that fact have important bearings on man's attitude toward his neighbor, it is the peace with God himself that is the basic Gospel message.

The author of Hebrews underscores the order of the titles of Melchizedek: "first . . . King of righteousness, and after that . . . King of peace" (7:2). Apart from God's righteousness, received by faith, there is no hope of genuine peace.

The reader of the Book of Genesis may be surprised that Melchizedek is "without father, without mother, without descent, having neither beginning of days, nor end of life" (7:3). Genesis is a book largely concerned with family lines and genealogies. We have lists of individuals among the descendants of Adam, Noah (and his three sons), Abraham, Ishmael, Esau, as well as the line from Abraham through Isaac and Jacob to the twelve tribes.

The reader of the Old Testament may also think it unusual that a man who did not have a proper genealogy could function as a priest. The priestly line in Israel was limited strictly to the family of Aaron. Even a king who presumed to usurp the functions of the priesthood was subject to censure.

The author of Hebrews tells us that the priesthood of Melchizedek was not dependent upon his family relationship. Genesis does not even mention the genealogy of Melchizedek (although, of course, as a man he had one). The Spirit of God caused the sacred historian to omit all references to Melchizedek's ancestors or his posterity. The record says nothing of "beginning of days" nor of "end of life." This that is true of the record of Melchizedek is true of the Person of Jesus. Although born in Bethlehem's manger at a definite time in history, Jesus is the One "whose goings forth have been from of old, from everlasting" (Mic. 5:2). His earthly life was taken from Him, in accord with the divine will, yet Jesus arose from the dead and declares, "I am he that liveth, and was dead; and, behold, I am alive forevermore" (Rev. 1:18).

2. *The superiority of Melchizedek to Aaron,* 7:4-10

The fact that Abraham was willing to pay tithes to Melchizedek is taken as a sign of the greatness of the priest-king of Salem (7:4). Abraham had been called of God to leave Ur, had been brought to Canaan, and had been promised the entire land as an inheritance. If anyone could have dispensed with the ministrations of Melchizedek, certainly Abraham could have. Yet the patriarch acknowledged the spiritual authority of this man by paying tithes to him.

Tithes, Hebrews reminds us (7:5), were normally given by the people to the sons of Levi "according to the law." The Mosaic Law laid down rules to govern the religious life of Israel in all its details. The acceptable sacrifices, the acceptable place of worship, and the acceptable priesthood were all specified.

Yet, Hebrews goes on to say, the Levitical priesthood of the Old Testament owes its origin to Abraham. Levi, one of the twelve sons of Jacob, actually "came out of the loins of Abraham" (7:5), and thus was a descendant of the patriarch.

The argument continues, however, that Melchizedek, who was not a Levitical priest (chronological considerations would rule out that possibility), received tithes from Abraham and blessed him (7:6). Since everyone knows that blessing comes from the greater to the lesser individual (7:7), we are to conclude that Melchizedek was greater than Abraham and, by extension, greater than Levi.

Since Levi in figure paid tithes to Melchizedek (7:9), the author of Hebrews concludes that the priesthood of Melchizedek must be superior to that of Aaron. The Levitical priesthood is composed of men who die (7:8), but the priesthood of Melchizedek contains no hint of death within it (7:8).

3. *The Aaronic priesthood superseded by that of Melchizedek,* 7:11-19

The argument from a comparison of the record of Melchizedek (in Genesis 14) with the Levitical priesthood finds further support in the words of Psalm 110:4: "The Lord hath sworn, and will not repent, Thou art a priest for ever after the order of Melchizedek." If the Levitical priesthood were perfect, why the reference to another priesthood (7:11)? Since priesthood was an integral part of the Mosaic Law, the acknowledgement that a change must be made in the priesthood will have far reaching consequences (7:12).

The Epistle to the Hebrews presents Christ as our great High Priest. The genealogy of Jesus, however, is through the tribe of Judah (7:14), a tribe which had no priestly responsibilities. How then could it be claimed that Jesus was a true priest? The answer is clear. The discussion of the priesthood of Melchizedek has all been preliminary to this statement. True, Jesus was not a Levitical priest, but He serves as priest of a more ancient and honorable order than that of Levi. He was a priest of the order of Melchizedek (7:15). The Levitical priesthood was established under the Law. It is described as part of a "carnal commandment" (7:16). The words are not meant to be derogatory. The Old Testament order is described in Hebrews as divine in origin but temporary in duration. It was carnal in the sense of "this-worldly." It met certain real needs among the people of God, but it was not meant to last forever. The very fact that prophecy speaks of another priesthood is enough to prove that the Levitical order will not last indefinitely.

The Old Testament sacrificial system, with its Levitical priesthood, is described as weak and unprofitable, or useless (7:18). It was weak because it could not actually make atonement for sin. It served a temporary function, but it served as a prophecy, looking forward to the sacrifice of Christ, and His ministration as High Priest after the order of Melchizedek.

Although the Law did not bring "perfection," i.e. it did not bring about the completion of God's purposes, it did introduce "a better hope" (7:19). The Law prepared for the Gospel. The ministrations of the Levitical priests testified to man's sinfulness and God's mercy. The Law caused sinful man to stand afar off. Through Christ, the "better hope," we now draw nigh to God with confidence.

4. *The superiority of Christ's priesthood,* 7:20-24

Psalm 110 is most emphatic in its presentation of the

priesthood of Melchizedek: "The Lord hath sworn, and will not repent." The priesthood of Christ was thus confirmed with the solemn oath of God (7:20-21). This fact should encourage the Christian. In the midst of the changing world, he trusts the changeless Christ who holds His office by virtue of the unalterable Word and will of God.

The Levitical priests were "many" (7:23). This was necessary because as creatures of time they were mortal. A succession had to be arranged so that there would always be someone to officiate at the altar. The priesthood of Christ is, however, eternal. He "continueth ever" (7:24) and is from age to age the same. It is for this reason that "he is able . . . to save them to the uttermost that come unto God by him, seeing he ever liveth to make intercession for them" (7:25). The resurrected Christ is enthroned at the Father's right hand. He is still concerned about His people. Although we think of the work of Christ as finished at Calvary, where atonement was made for sin, we should remember the continuing ministry of the resurrected Christ, our Advocate with the Father.

5. *Christ, the Priest who meets our needs,* 7:25-28

This High Priest "became" us (7:26). This is but another way of saying that Jesus is a suitable, a fitting High Priest. In the economy of God, Jesus was the One ordained to meet the needs of His people. He is "holy, harmless, undefiled, separate from sinners, and made higher than the heavens" (7:26). Because of this He can be trusted. His perfect righteousness gives Him unchallenged rights to the Father's presence. His position "higher than the heavens" reminds us that He is accepted at the throne of grace and ever beloved of the Father.

The Old Testament priesthood offered a daily succession of sacrifices. Priests made offerings for themselves and then for the people (7:27). Those priests were themselves sinful men, and they are here contrasted with the spotless Son of God. Christ made one sacrifice; He offered Himself, and that sacrifice was one of infinite merit. The thought of adding to it is actually blasphemy.

The priesthood under the Mosaic Law was one of infirmity (7:28). Although all must be physically sound and ceremonially purified at the laver before approaching the sanctuary, still these men never lost sight of the fact that they were sinners. In contrast to the weakness of the Old Testament priesthood stands the strength of the Son—consecrated, perfected forever. He had no blemish that needed to be atoned for; He presented Himself to God in all the beauty of His perfection.

F. CHRIST THE TRUE HIGH PRIEST, 8:1—10:18

1. *His entrance into the true Sanctuary*, 8:1-5

The Epistle to the Hebrews began with the statement, "God . . . hath . . . spoken." Here we read another solemn, yet blessed affirmation, "We have . . . an high priest" (8:1). Judaism had a priesthood which functioned in the Temple at Jerusalem in accord with the directions contained in the Mosaic Law. The Christian, however, has all that was enjoyed under the Old Covenant—and more. He has "an high priest, who is set on the right hand of the throne of the Majesty in the heavens" (8:1).

The place in which the heavenly High Priest ministers may be contrasted with the earthly Tabernacle which served as the sanctuary for Israel before the erecting of Solomon's Temple. The earthly structure is not the "true tabernacle," however (8:2), because it was pitched by man. The men who built the Tabernacle were directed by the Holy Spirit in their labors, but they were still earthly creatures and their work bore the marks of human sin. Glorious as it was, it was not the true abode of God. Although God revealed Himself in glory between the two cherubim in the Holy of Holies, no discerning Israelite thought that God could be contained within that structure. Solomon spoke with understanding when he said, "The heaven of heavens cannot contain thee" (I Kings 8:27).

The High Priest, by virtue of his office, approached God with a sacrifice. In this respect his ministry differed from that of the prophet. The prophet stood before the people as God's representative. The priest stood before God, representing the people. Prayer and sacrifice were his prime responsibilities.

The specific sphere of the priestly ministry of Jesus is defined as Heaven itself. At the time of the writing of Hebrews, the Temple was still standing, and priests who traced their lineage back to Aaron offered sacrifices there day by day. This was not the ministry which Jesus had while on earth, however. He was concerned with the reality, while those priests were working among the shadows (8:4-5).

God's word to Moses at Mount Sinai may be cited to show the heavenly origin of the true Tabernacle. God said "See . . . that thou make all things according to the pattern shewed to thee in the mount" (8:5). The revelation of the Sanctuary had come from Heaven. Men on earth, following directions which were given by God, built the structure but the structure they built was not the true Sanctuary. That which they built was the "shadow of heavenly things."

Another direct revelation had been made from Heaven in the Person of Jesus. He "dwelt" (lit. "tabernacled") among men who bore witness to the fact that they saw "his glory" (John 1:14). Jesus was the "substance" of which the Tabernacle was but a shadow. He was not a reflection of heavenly reality, but God Himself, entering our humanity—Immanuel, God with us.

2. *Christ as Priest of the New Covenant, 8:6-13*

The ministry of Jesus, then, is "more excellent" (8:6) than any ministry of a son of Aaron in the earthly Sanctuary. The Person of the priest, and the nature of the Sanctuary both argue for the superiority of the heavenly High Priest, who is enthroned at the Father's right hand.

The relationship which Israel sustained to God is described in terms of a covenant. At Sinai, Israel accepted the Law, including its priesthood and system of sacrifice. Yet that Law had not been effective in stemming the evil desires of God's people. During the years in the wilderness, they persistently murmured against God and His servant, Moses. After they entered Canaan, they fell prey to the gods of the land. Licentious Baal worship became common in Israel. Although there were times of spiritual revival, sparked by pious kings such as Hezekiah and Josiah, the general tendency was toward apostasy. Israel's God saw fit to take first the Northern Kingdom, Israel, and, a century and a half later, the Southern Kingdom, Judah, into exile. God had been faithful to

His people, but again and again they had turned their backs upon Him. There was nothing wrong with His Law, but there was much wrong with His people, who persisted in rebellion. Paul says that the Law was weak "through the flesh." Sinful man would not obey it.

Just as there had been the promise of a new priesthood—a priest "after the order of Melchizedek," so God had prophesied a new covenant through the prophet Jeremiah (Jer. 31:31-34). The same logic which applied to the priesthood can apply to the covenant. If the first covenant had been faultless, there would have been no need for the promise of a second (8:7). Yet God through Jeremiah offered a message of hope to the generation which was going into exile. They had proved faithless to Israel's God. Jeremiah complained that they had as many gods as they had cities. He insisted that God would send them into exile, where they would remain for seventy years. Yet, Jeremiah did not end on a note of despair. God would one day write a new covenant, not on tablets of stone, but on the fleshly tablets of the human heart. Man's inner motivation would be transformed. He would become a new creature.

The first covenant is described in very tender tones. God had taken His people "by the hand" to lead them out of Egypt (8:9). They had cried to Him because of their oppressors, and He had proved Himself to be the God who cared for His own. Yet there was something basically wrong. Sin prevailed, and Israel had to be solemnly disciplined.

A new situation would take place, however "after those days" (8:10). The laws would be written on the hearts of the people, and God could say, "I will be to them a God, and they shall be to me a people." This is in brief the nature of the covenant. The Sovereign God agreed to care for His dependent people. They had but the duty to enthrone Him in their hearts.

The words of verse eleven may not be fully realized until we shall see our Lord and be like Him, but they are meant to be true of us here and now: "And they shall not teach every man his neighbor, and every man his brother, saying, Know the Lord: for all shall know me, from the least to the greatest." The people of God shall have personal knowledge of Him. His Spirit permanently abides with them (John 14:17).

One of the great doctrines which was reemphasized at the time of the Protestant Reformation was that of the priesthood of believers. Every Christian, related by faith to Jesus Christ, has the right of priestly access to God in prayer. Some believers know more about the Lord than their less instructed brethren, but the weakest Christian truly "knows" the Lord. We may honor human teachers as gifts of Christ to his church, but we need not be dependent upon them.

The New Covenant does what the Old Covenant could never do; it provides a final atonement for sin: "Their sins and their iniquities will I remember no more" (8:12). The consciousness of sin was never wholly obliterated by the Old Covenant:

> Not all the blood of beasts,
>   On Jewish altars slain,
> Could give the guilty conscience peace,
>   Or wash away the stain.

But Christ, the heavenly Lamb,
Takes all our sins away—
A sacrifice of nobler name
And richer blood than they.

Under the Old Covenant a remembrance of sin was perpetuated year after year. There were daily offerings, sacrifices for the new moons and sabbaths, and a solemn Day of Atonement when sin was again remembered and ceremonially removed. This, according to Hebrews, is now forever past. Sins are forgotten by the God of all grace. There is no fear of condemnation to the child of God.

The author of Hebrews was conscious of the momentous days in which he lived. They were "these last days" (1:2) in which God had spoken in His Son. They were also days in which the Jewish priesthood which had served from time immemorial was about to be changed. The entire covenant, entered by Israel at Sinai, was now becoming obsolete and growing old. It was "ready to vanish away" (8:13).

This was not wishful thinking or polemical writing. As a matter of historical fact, within a short time after these lines were penned, the city of Jerusalem with its Temple which Herod had beautified was in ruins. The armies of the Roman general, Titus, entered Jerusalem and put an end to a whole era of Jewish life. The Temple was destroyed, and it has not been restored. Today the Temple site is occupied by a Moslem mosque known as the Dome of the Rock. Pious Jews have continued to study the minutiae of the Mosaic Law, but no priest offers a sacrifice today. The old order is gone. The first covenant indeed has vanished away.

3. *The old Tabernacle and its services,* 9:1-7

The first covenant, that of Mount Sinai, had "ordinances of divine service, and a worldly sanctuary" (9:1). Services were prescribed by God and they were conducted in the Tabernacle here, in this world. The Sanctuary was actually in two parts. Entering from the court, the priest would first come to the Holy Place, which contained a seven-branched candlestick and a table containing "shewbread," or "bread of the Presence." The candlestick was actually a candelabrum with seven oil lamps which illuminated the Holy Place. The twelve loaves of shewbread represented the tribes of Israel within the Sanctuary of the Lord.

The priest entered through a veil from the court to the Holy Place. Once a year, on the Day of Atonement, the high priest penetrated the second veil (9:3) which separated the Holy Place from the Most Holy Place (or "Holy of Holies"). Here was the sacred ark of the covenant, the most sacred object related to the faith of early Israel. Surmounting the ark were two golden cherubim, facing one another. The lid of the ark was known as the mercy seat. There, on the Day of Atonement, the high priest sprinkled the sacrificial blood which he brought into the Holy of Holies. Within the ark in ancient times was a golden pot of manna (Exod. 16:33), the rod of Aaron which had miraculously budded during the wilderness wandering (Num. 17:10), and the two tablets of the Law (cf. I Kings 8:9).

Priests daily entered the Holy Place, but the Holy of Holies was the throne room of Israel's God, and He sought to impress the sanctity of His Person upon His people by means of very explicit directions. It was not possible for just anyone to approach the sacred ark. This was the prerogative of the one who was divinely chosen, the son of Aaron who served as High Priest. The High Priest did not have continuous access to the Holy of Holies, however. He entered, with a bloody sacrifice, but once a year (9:7). The blood was offered both for his own sins and for those of his people. Actually the blood came from two animals: a bullock, prescribed for the High Priest, and a goat, prescribed for the people.

4. *Ineffectiveness of the sacrifices of the old Tabernacle,* 9:8-10

The ceremonial observances of the Old Covenant are not cited because of antiquarian interest. God used them to teach important lessons to His people. During the days of the Tabernacle, a series of curtains kept the ordinary Israelite and, indeed, the ordinary priest from entering the Holy of Holies. God was impressing upon His people both their own sinfulness and His holiness. They learned that the sinner could not, apart from some fresh work of grace, ever hope to see God.

The difficulty associated with worship at the Tabernacle and its successor, the Temple, was its concern with externals. Sacrifices were offered, but they "could not make him that did the service perfect, as pertaining to the conscience" (9:9). They were external and temporal rather than internal and eternal. They served as a figure, or a symbol, for the generations which they served. As such they were types of the better ministry of Christ.

Verse 10 describes the Old Testament rites as "meats and drinks, and divers washings, and carnal ordinances, imposed on them until the time of reformation." The word translated "reformation" is used as a medical term for the setting of a fracture. It speaks of putting things right. The world is presented to us as "out of joint," and only as Christ enters a life is there a true rectification—a making things right. The Old Testament looked forward in hope to that day. In type and in prophecy, God was stating that He would send His Messiah—His Anointed One—Who would bring about the consummation of all history.

5. *Superiority of Christ's sacrifice,* 9:11-14

We confidently declare now that Christ has come! The best Greek texts read not that Jesus is the priest of "good things to come" but, rather, "of good things which have come to pass" (9:11). Although it is true that the Christian has much to look forward to, even now he is a child of God, and should rejoice in His abundant provision for all needs. Christ now ministers not in an earthly structure but in the heavenly Temple. The Holy Place into which He entered (9:12) was not one into which the blood of bulls and goats, mere figures of spiritual realities, might be brought. Jesus "by his own blood . . . entered in once . . . having obtained eternal redemption" (9:12).

The author of Hebrews again presents us with a series of contrasts. The Levitical priests entered an earthly Tabernacle; Jesus an heavenly one. They brought the blood of bulls and goats; He, His own blood. They entered many times; He but once. They could bring no permanent cure for man's spiritual ills; He "obtained eternal redemption."

The blood of bulls and goats did, in the Old Testament economy, "sanctify" in an external way (9:13). Man was rendered ceremonially pure after the priest had conducted the prescribed ritual. He could take his place in Israel and function as a normal member of the chosen nation. Yet the blood of Christ has infinitely greater efficacy than any of the Old Testament sacrifices. He "through the eternal Spirit offered himself without spot to God" (9:14). Christ willingly submitted to the death of the Cross. He was both the High Priest and the offering. Because of His sinless life He had no need of sacrifices for Himself. His death made atonement for His people. His sinlessness rendered Him the sacrifice "without spot."

This sacrifice is able to "purge your conscience from dead works to serve the living God" (9:14). This is a practical reality. The sacrifice of Christ gives the believer a position before God, so that we may say that he is justified. It provides a righteousness which is imputed to the believer, and it also imparts a power to the believer so that "dead works" are purged away. The works of the spiritually dead man are "dead works," but the newborn Christian now has a divine power whereby he is enabled "to serve the living God." In his own strength, the believer is no more able to serve God than the sinner was able to save himself. All of the graces which the Spirit bestows on us find their basis in the work of Christ. It is because the blood was shed that we can now, depending on the Spirit, serve God.

6. *The Mediator of the New Covenant,* 9:15-28

The sacrificial offering of Christ, in contrast to the Old

Testament offerings of bulls and goats, marked the beginning of a New Covenant, or Testament. Moses had been the mediator of the covenant at Sinai. God revealed Himself to Moses who, in turn, gave the Law to Israel and consecrated Aaron and his sons for the priestly ministry. Christ, however, by the offering of Himself became the Mediator of the New Covenant. At the Last Supper Jesus said to His disciples, "This cup is the new testament [or covenant] in my blood, which is shed for you" (Luke 22:20).

The death of Christ accomplished "the redemption of the transgressions that were under the first covenant" (9:15). Although distinct, the two covenants are related. The old typified and prophesied the new. Those who had sinned under the Old Covenant might now find mercy. In contrast to the temporary results of the sacrifices made under the first covenant, Christ has accomplished "eternal redemption" for His people.

Some confusion exists in the English translations of the Greek word *diatheke*, which means both covenant and testament. When used as a covenant, however, it does not imply that the parties to the covenant are equals. God, at Sinai, was the Sovereign whose Law was mediated to the people through Moses. A *diatheke* is, in this sense, a covenant in which an individual may dispose of his property as he sees fit. This use of the word is not far removed from the idea of a will, or testament. In ancient times such covenants, or testaments, were usually solemnized by the offering of animal sacrifices.

The author of Hebrews notes that a testament has no force until the death of the testator (9:16-17). The covenant-testament at Sinai was consecrated with the blood of sacrificial victims (9:18-23; Exod. 24:3-8). This service was in accord with God's specific command (9:20). Blood was sprinkled on the sacred book of the covenant, the people (9:19), the Tabernacle itself, and its furnishings (9:21). Blood was so prominent in the service that the principle could be enunciated: "Without shedding of blood is no remission" (9:22).

These rites were performed in the "patterns of things in the heavens" (9:23). Approach to the heavenly reality must be even more solemn! On behalf of sinful man Jesus the great High Priest entered Heaven itself. The earthly "holy places made with hands" (9:24) were but symbols of the heavenly abode. A sacrifice better than that of bulls and goats was needed there (9:23).

The high priest entered the earthly sanctuary "often," i.e. once every year (9:25). He brought the blood of others, namely the animals prescribed in the Mosaic Law. Christ, however, entered the true Tabernacle (Heaven itself) once, and He Himself was the sacrificial victim (9:26). As man dies once (9:27), so Christ died once (9:28). His people—those who look for Him—shall see Him at His coming again.

Sin has been atoned for, the believer is justified! This is the Gospel proclamation. On the Cross Jesus cried, "It is finished" (John 19:30). Christ was offered "once" to "bear the sins of many." At His second coming He will not deal with sin again, for that has already been removed. Then He shall bring about the consummation of all things as He reigns as sovereign over His redeemed people.

7. *Weakness of the sacrifices of the Law,* 10:1-5

As Christ the Son was superior to the prophets of the Old Testament, and as the priesthood of Melchizedek was superior to that of Aaron, so the entire ceremonial law of the Old Testament is described as a "shadow" (10:1) of the "good things to come" through the priestly ministry of Christ. The Saviour was the "reality" of which the Levitical priests were the "shadow." The Law, we read, was "not the very image of the things." The true form of the spiritual realities awaited the fullness of times when the Saviour appeared. As a shadow the Law served to prepare men's hearts for the reality, but after Jesus came the shadows would no longer be meaningful. The annual repetition of the Levitical offerings was itself evidence that there was nothing final about them.

The worshiper who brought his sacrifice to the Tabernacle or the Temple did not leave with the thought that his problems were solved. He had performed the prescribed rite, but he carried with him a continuing consciousness of sin. He knew it would be necessary to return again and again. The guilt of sin lay heavy on the sinner.

The reason it was necessary to repeat the Old Testament sacrifices is not hard to find: "It is not possible that the blood of bulls and of goats should take away sins" (10:4). They served a temporary function, but they pointed to the need of a greater sacrifice. Jesus came as the Lamb of God who purposed to take away the sin of the world. He was named Jesus because He was destined to take upon Himself the sin of His people.

8. *The incarnation,* 10:6-9

Indeed, the Old Testament itself testifies to the fact
that offerings prescribed by the Law cannot bring righteousness. The mission of Christ is summarized in the
words of Psalm 40:7-9: "Wherefore when he cometh into the world, he saith, Sacrifice and offering thou would-
est not, but a body hast thou prepared me: In burnt-
offerings and sacrifices for sin thou hast had no pleasure. Then said I, Lo, I come (in the volume of the book
it is written of me,) to do thy will, O God" (10:5-7).

The principal difference between the passage in Psalm
40 and the quotation from it in Hebrews 10 is the expression in the latter, "a body hast thou prepared
me." The Hebrew text of Psalm 40 reads, "mine ear hast
thou opened." The Greek translators of the Psalter in-
troduced a paraphrase: "ears hast thou prepared for me."
In both instances the emphasis is on obedience. The
speaker has an ear, open to hear the commands of the
Lord. His ear is prepared to hear and respond. In apply-
ing these words to Christ, the author of Hebrews extended the concept of ears to the entire body. The obedient Son of God had a body, prepared by the Father, in
which He would always do the Father's will.

The quotation from the Psalm had a negative element.
God did not have pleasure in sacrifices which were offered in accord with the commands of the Mosaic Law
(10:8) apart from an attitude of faith. The "pleasure"
here is the satisfaction that comes from a finished work.
There is no question that the Old Testament sacrifices
were ordained of God. They were designed to serve as
a type and prophecy of the offering of Christ. In the

eternal purpose of God, the offering of the blood of His Son could alone avail to cleanse from sin, and redemption was completed only when He bore the sins of His people on Calvary's Cross.

The words of Christ, "Lo, I come to do thy will, O God" (10:9), are properly contrasted with the Old Testament sacrifices. They did not avail to put away sin; He came to do the will of the Father. Lest there be any question concerning the import of Christ's ministry a principle is enunciated: "He taketh away the first, that he may establish the second" (10:9). The author of Hebrews argues that it is "either or" not "both and." It is not possible to come to God by means of the blood of bulls and goats prescribed at Sinai and the Lamb of God who died on Calvary! The first covenant, that made at Sinai, is specifically rejected. It served its purpose, but that purpose is no longer a valid one. Christ through His death has become the Mediator of a New Covenant, and He is our only hope.

Although these words had specific reference to the ancient Hebrew Christians who received the letter, their application is universal. Every effort apart from Jesus Christ to win the favor of God is futile. The Mosaic Law could not bring peace to the guilty conscience, and neither can any other legal system, whether it goes under the name of Christianity or paganism.

> Could my zeal no languor know,
>   Could my tears forever flow,
> These for sin could not atone.
>   Thou must save, and Thou alone.

9. *The one satisfactory offering,* 10:10-18

Emphasis is placed on the fact that the offering of Jesus is "once for all" (10:10). The Saviour offered one perfect sacrifice to sanctify, i.e. to set apart to Himself a people who would be redeemed from sin and share His eternal glory. To suggest that other sacrifices be added to this one great sacrifice would be to question its merit. Christ, in His death, accomplished that which God had willed, and all other sacrifices were rendered meaningless.

Human priests offer the same type of offerings day after day (10:11), and they never can bring peace to a single troubled soul. As day follows day the sinner approaches despair. He is powerless to cleanse his own soul, and the blood of animals shed at the altar does him no good. Christ, however, changes all that. He offered "one sacrifice" (10:12) which is eternally efficacious. The sinner can now be assured that he will not again be confronted with the evidence of guilt. In Christ atonement has been completed. The Priest does not need to stand within the Holy Place again. Our great High Priest is now seated "on the right hand of God" (10:12).

The resurrected Christ will one day be universally worshiped as the Lord of Glory. The powers of darkness have not yet been subdued, but He is now waiting "till his enemies be made his footstool" (10:13). The Father has said to Him, "Ask of me, and I shall give thee the heathen for thine inheritance, and the uttermost parts of the earth for thy possession. Thou shalt break them with a rod of iron; thou shalt dash them in pieces like a potter's vessel" (Ps. 2:8-9).

Although the enemies of Christ may properly fear His wrath, those who avail themselves of His mercy are assured of safety. The one sacrifice will forever avail (10:14). The man in Christ will never stand condemned. "Who shall separate us from the love of Christ? shall tribulation, or distress, or persecution, or famine, or nakedness, or peril, or sword? . . . Nay, in all these things we are more than conquerors through him that loved us" (Rom. 8:35-37). Christ said, "I will build my church; and the gates of hell shall not prevail against it" (Matt. 16:18). The Christian may be assailed by "principalities and powers," and all the might of the evil one, but he is safe because the sacrifice of Jesus avails eternally.

The witness of the Old Testament to these facts should give us further grounds of confidence in the wisdom and power of God. Redemption was not an afterthought but a part of the divine program for the ages. Jeremiah spoke of the day when God would make a New Covenant with His people, writing His law on their hearts and minds (10:16; Jer. 31:33). The result is the divine assurance, "Their sins and iniquities will I remember no more" (10:17).

If sins are not remembered, there is no need to make an offering for them. God declares that He has forgotten them and man is not to continue to stagger under their burden. The Levitical offerings are unnecessary now (10:18), for the believer is assured that Christ has removed his sins from him as far as the east is removed from the west.

IV

PRACTICAL EXHORTATIONS

10:19–13:25

A. Drawing Near To God and Holding Fast the Faith, 10:19-23

In view of the perfect sacrifice of Christ, the believer can now approach God without fear. The term "boldness" (10:19) does not suggest irreverence. We are, and always shall be, the creatures of God, dependent upon Him for all that we are and have. He has provided, however, through the sacrificial death of His Son a means by which we can approach His very presence. Old Testament Israel had to stand afar off. We are now urged to approach the throne of grace with confidence, because He desires fellowship with His redeemed people. It is "by the blood of Jesus" that we enter "the holiest." High Priests of old brought animal blood into the Holy of Holies once a year, but we daily approach Heaven itself with the blood of the Saviour as our confidence.

Our means of access to God is "a new and living way" (10:20). It is new, in contrast to the Mosaic offerings which were not only old but also antiquated, ready to "pass away." It is a "living way" because our High Priest, the Mediator of the New Covenant, is forever alive. We do not now approach God with a lifeless animal but through the living Christ. The Old Testament priest entered through a veil into the Holy of Holies. In like manner we enter God's presence through a veil, but it is the veil of the flesh of the Son of God, which was pierced by wicked men and now gives us access to God. In His incarnation, Jesus took upon Himself a true human nature. The very piercing of His body, however, was the means used by God to provide an entrance for sinners into His presence. Even within the Jerusalem Temple, the veil was rent in twain at the time of the crucifixion (Matt. 27:51). The Old Testament rites had been powerless to open the way of access to God, but Jesus had done so finally and irrevocably when His body was pierced for us.

It is, of course, one thing to be told that the work of Christ is completely efficacious, and another so to trust Him that life is freed from the bondage and frustrations of an evil conscience. The Christian Gospel affirms that God has done certain things for us. It then asks us to believe God and act upon all that He has done.

Since Christ has done so much for us, we are urged to "draw near with a true heart in full assurance of faith" (10:22). Those accustomed to the Old Testament ritual might hesitate to do this. Then the emphasis was upon the fact of sin as an offence to God. Now there is a new emphasis. Hateful as sin is, Jesus has taken it from us, and we need not fear God. We can and should confidently approach the throne of God and acknowledge ourselves His children. To refuse to do so is actually to spurn His grace and to insult the God and Father of our

Lord Jesus Christ. We do not come boldly to Him because we are now better than others, but because Jesus
has made full atonement for our sins.

In the Old Testament approach to God, the priest
sprinkled blood in the sanctuary. Through faith in Christ
our hearts have been "sprinkled from an evil conscience"
(10:22). Christ has atoned for our guilt. His blood has
been applied, by faith, to our wicked hearts. As we draw
near we do so with bodies "washed with pure water"
(10:22). The Old Testament priest ceremonially cleansed
himself at the laver before entering the Tabernacle where
he performed his sacred ministrations. We must be
cleansed as we approach the throne of grace, but God
has provided a laver of cleansing in the blood of Jesus
Christ which cleanses from all sin (I John 1:7). The rite
of Christian baptism symbolically represented this in-
ward cleansing which is indispensable for fellowship
with God.

The priesthood of all believers is a truth stressed in
these verses. All believers now may enter "the holiest"
(10:19) passing through "the veil" (10:20), and approaching God Himself through Jesus Christ (10:21-22).
All believers know the meaning of cleansing at the laver
and the sprinkling of the blood upon the heart. God had
said of Israel, "Ye shall be unto me a kingdom of priests,
and an holy nation" (Exod. 19:6), and Peter said of the
Church, "Ye are a chosen generation, a royal priesthood,
an holy nation" (I Peter 2:9). All who name the name
of Christ have the right of priestly access to God.

The believer-priest in times of trial has a twofold responsibility. Because God is faithful, we should "hold
fast the confession of our hope" (10:23). The words

"profession of our faith" (A.V.) are not strictly accurate. Of course we do "profess faith," but the words here used speak of confession, public witness to our confidence in God, and hope, faith in its forward look. As believers we know that God holds the key to the future. "If God be for us, who can be against us?" (Rom. 8:31).

B. CHRISTIAN RESPONSIBILITY AND GOD'S JUDGMENTS, 10:24-31

Personal confession is to be augmented by a concern for our brethren: "Let us consider one another to provoke unto love and to good works" (10:24). A constant and helpful concern for fellow Christians is the responsibility of every child of God. We do not live to ourselves. It is possible to encourage one another in the things of Christ. An attitude of love should be the goal of all our Christian activities. "Good works" are the fruit of salvation rather than its cause (Eph. 2:8-10), but they should not be despised. God working within us will enable us to do those things which are well pleasing in His sight.

The Christian witness is not a private matter but normally finds expression in the church. We should not forsake "the assembling of ourselves together, as the manner of some is" (10:25). The testimony, prayer, and fellowship of an assembly of believers accords to all benefits which should never be overlooked. Although we should be willing to stand alone if necessary, God usually brings His children together into assemblies where they may labor and pray together. This is particularly important because we actually need one another. No Christian has all the gifts of the Spirit. We are members of Christ's body: "For the body is not one member, but many. . . .

And the eye cannot say unto the hand, I have no need of thee: nor again the head to the feet, I have no need of you. . . . Now ye are the body of Christ, and members in particular" (I Cor. 12:14-27).

Consistency in fellowship and exhortation is encouraged "so much the more as ye see the day approaching" (10:25). The readers of the Epistle to the Hebrews were living in the tragic days just before the destruction of Jerusalem. Important changes were in store both for them and for the unbelieving Jews. In such times it was both wise and proper for Christians to remain together, exercising a united testimony to the Gospel. Our own generation also has seen momentous events. Although we do not know the day or the hour when the Saviour shall return, history appears to be reaching a climax. When the twentieth century arrived, many thought that we were about to embark on a golden age—a man-made millennium. The passing of the years has not only dulled that hope but put it into reverse. Man now fears annihilation. The exhortation to Christian steadfastness was never more needed than at the present hour. Believers may not always agree on certain details of their faith, but as believers they must be ready to make common cause against the enemy of their souls. We may not know what the immediate future will hold, but we do know that one day the kingdoms of this world will become the kingdoms of our Lord and His Christ. Here is a basis for steadfast hope in a generation which knows the meaning of fear.

The consequences of willfully rejecting God's grace are frightful to consider: "For if we sin wilfully after that we have received the knowledge of the truth, there remaineth no more sacrifice for sins" (10:26). Is it possi-

ble for the one who rejects Christ to go back to the "blood
of bulls and goats" as a means of atonement? The answer is, "No!" The one who dares to reject Christ has no
place to which to turn. He has spurned his only hope
for time and eternity. For him there is "a certain fearful
looking for of judgment and fiery indignation, which
shall devour the adversaries" (10:27). It may be ironical,
but Christ is the Saviour of those who are saved and the
Judge of those who are judged. Mercy is freely offered,
but if mercy is spurned, the sinner must face the wrath
of Almighty God.

Again analogies may be drawn from the Old Testament: "He that despised Moses' law died without mercy
under two or three witnesses" (10:28; cf. Deut. 17:6).
The Old Testament offered mercy to the sinner who
brought his offering to the Tabernacle (Lev. 1:1-4). Although such acts could not bring more than a temporary
and ceremonial renewal of divine favor, they were expressive of a believing heart. The one who sinned with
an high hand in open defiance of God experienced no
mercy.

If, however, such punishment was meted out to the
individual who sinned against the lesser revelation of
God in the Old Testament, what can we expect of the
judgment of God upon the one who rejects the final
revelation in His Son? Such defiance is a treading under
foot of the Son of God, a despising of the blood of the
New Covenant, an outrage against the Holy Spirit, here
named the Spirit of Grace (10:29).

This is not the picture of a child of God who has
temporarily fallen into sin. This is the man who blatant-
ly denies Christ and rejects the salvation which God has

provided. Christ makes it clear that He will not break the bruised reed (Matt. 12:20). The rebel, however, is treated differently: "Vengeance belongeth unto me, I will recompense, saith the Lord" (10:30). God as the judge upholds the moral law (Deut. 32:35). This applied even to Israel: "The Lord shall judge his people" (Ps. 135:14).

This solemn reminder of the fearful consequences of sin closes with a warning: "It is a fearful thing to fall into the hands of the living God" (10:31). God takes no delight in the death of the wicked. He is the God of all grace. Yet He is the God of holiness who must punish sin. Those who have fled for refuge to the Saviour have found peace and security. Those who chose to pursue their own sinful paths of rejection and defiance must stand before the Judge of all the earth.

C. PAST FAITHFULNESS A GROUND FOR PRESENT CONFIDENCE, 10:32-39

The Hebrews, however, had enjoyed periods of spiritual triumph. The remembrance of these should serve as a stimulus to faithfulness in fresh difficulties. They had "endured a great fight of afflictions" (32), a hard struggle in which they were called upon to suffer. God had given grace at that earlier time, even when they were publicly exposed to abuse—"made a gazingsstock" (10:33). On other occasions they were partners to those who were called upon to suffer for the Gospel. This took grace, for it would be easy to dissociate themselves from those who by their Christian testimony had incurred the wrath of the civil leaders. Yet these Hebrews had been willing to share in the trials of those who were suffering for the sake of Christ.

The recipients of the Epistle to the Hebrews had shown compassion toward those who were imprisoned for the testimony of Jesus Christ. The oldest Greek texts do not justify the reading, "Ye had compassion of me in my bonds" (10:34). Delitzsch reads, "Ye . . . showed a fellow-feeling for them that were in bonds." This showed itself in a practical way. The enemies of Christ plundered the property of the Christians, but they accepted it without complaining. Since their true riches were in Heaven, they did not mourn their loss of earthly goods.

This had been the glorious history of the Hebrews. They had begun well. They had a confidence in God which was directed toward the future. The things of time and sense might pass; they lived in the light of eternity. The writer urges them: "Cast not away . . . your confidence" (10:35).

Their immediate need was patience. They were in danger of growing "weary in well doing." The word rendered "patience" (10:36) means, "remaining under the load." We might call it endurance. Do not try to shirk your responsibility. Continue to serve the Lord faithfully. He will give relief in due time.

The hope of the struggling one is the appearance of the Lord: "For yet a little while, and he that shall come will come, and will not tarry" (10:37). This hope was held forth in the Old Testament (Hab. 2:3). God does not delay without cause. If the night seems long, be of good cheer; the day is at hand, He is still in sovereign control.

Amid the trials there is one means of life: "Now the just shall live by faith" (10:38; Hab. 2:4). Bible scholars have long discussed the meaning of the Hebrew word rendered "faith" in the Habakkuk passage. Some would translate it, "The just shall live by his faithfulness." However the word is translated, the meaning is not basically different. The faithful man is the one who lays hold of the faithfulness of God. The one who draws back (10:38) denies the faith and shows a lack of faithfulness. The one requirement of stewards is that they be found faithful (I Cor. 4:2).

The author of the epistle associates himself with his readers in the observation, "We are not of them who draw back unto perdition; but of them that believe to the saving of the soul" (10:39). True believers press on with the full assurance of faith. Trials serve to divide those who merely profess faith from those whose lives are actually built on the firm foundation of Christian reality. It cannot be denied that there have been many who have professed faith in Christ who have subsequently turned back. John speaks of such: "They went out from us, but they were not of us; for if they had been of us, they would no doubt have continued with us: but they went out, that they might be made manifest that they were not all of us" (I John 2:19).

D. The Household of Faith, 11:1-40

1. *Characteristics of faith,* 11:1-3

The guiding principle of the Christian life is faith. This is not simply a psychological factor, however. To some people faith means believing that you can do a job better than you have done it in the past, or believing that a loved one will rise from his bed of sickness. There may be real value in such "positive thinking," but this is not the meaning of faith. True Biblical faith has God as its object. We believe God and trust His Word. That Word does not tell us that we have any reason to expect to be the richest merchant on Main Street. It tells us, on the contrary, that we will have tribulations and that as Jesus' disciples we will have crosses to bear. It assures us, however, of grace to bear them. Faith has a backward look. It declares that God has done mighty acts in days gone by. Faith also has a forward look. It declares that He can be trusted for the future.

Although Scripture does not define faith, a number of things are stated about it. "Faith," we read (11:1), "is the substance of things hoped for, the evidence of things not seen." The word translated "substance" was used in the sense of "title deed" in apostolic times. Faith is the firm assurance, the conviction, that God will do what He has promised to do. It would, of course, be presumption to insist that He must do what we want done. Many Christians grow disillusioned in their Christian lives because God does not conform to their wills. Faith takes God at His word; faith does not insist that He conform to our ideas.

Many of the Hebrews were growing restless because they did not see God solving their immediate problems. It is a temptation to a Christian to reason, "God doesn't love me," when the answer to his prayers is delayed. "Faith," however, "is the evidence [literally, "proof"] of things not seen." It is the conviction that God knows what He is doing, even when we don't!

If it seems irrational to exercise such faith, history provides ample justification for it: "by it the elders obtained a good report" (11:2). We are at the end of a long line of faithful men, and each of them found that God was worthy of his trust. These men would be unknown to us today except for the fact that they trusted God.

The material universe is understandable only on the basis of faith. How did it come into being? By the creative word of God. He said, "Let there be light: and there was light" (Gen. 1:3). Faith sees God as the prime Source and responsible Agent in creation. He brought into being that which previously did not exist: "things which are seen were not made of things which do appear" (11:3). Faith may not understand all of the processes by which the world was brought to its present condition, but it sees God behind them all. Faith may not know how long it took God to create the present world, but it rests in God as Creator.

2. *Examples of faith*, 11:4-32

The heroes of faith begin with a martyr. It was "by faith" that Abel offered "a more excellent sacrifice than Cain" (11:4). The author of Hebrews does not allude to the difference in the offerings themselves. Cain had brought from the fruit of his fields an offering to God, but Abel took "of the firstlings of his flock" (Gen. 4:3-4). Both cared for the externals of religion, but only one was accepted. The offering "by faith" was an offering which had been made in accord with the revealed will of God. Cain made the mistake of reasoning that his offering was "just as good." He thought he was doing the best he could. Yet religious observances which are not in accord with God's revealed will are based on superstition, not on faith.

God accepted the offering of Abel, yet He did not

prevent his brother from killing him! Men who look for their rewards in this world are often disappointed. Although a martyr, Abel's life was not lived in vain: "He being dead yet speaketh" (11:4). Abel shows us that the life of faith may be a rugged one, but the smile of God is what really matters.

A second antediluvian saint is Enoch (11:5). We know only one thing about the life of Enoch—"He pleased God." His biography, found in Gen. 5:21-24, occupies but a few lines. "And Enoch walked with God: and he was not; for God took him." This was the life of faith. Whether or not he accomplished great things is beside the point. Jude tells us that he was a prophet (Jude 14-15), yet no mention of that is made by the author of Hebrews. The most important thing that can be said of him is that he pleased God.

Enoch left this world in a way different from others: "By faith Enoch was translated that he should not see death" (11:5). One day the faithful man could not be found. He had lived for eternity rather than for time, and God miraculously took him away. The same pattern does not apply to all men of faith. There is a variety in God's dealings with His children. Each, however, is under the protecting care of God.

The constituent elements in faith are few, but there is no substitute for them. The man of faith believes in the existence of God (11:6). He may or may not know a great deal about this God. After Jesus had healed a man who was born blind, the man testified, "Whether he be a sinner or no, I know not: one thing I know, that, whereas I was blind, now I see" (John 9:25). It is possible for us to have many false conceptions about God and still be men of faith. We must, however, believe Him.

The God whom we believe is not an abstract "first cause," but a personal Being. He is "a rewarder of them that diligently seek him" (11:6). Faith is thus an active element of life. It not only passively waits on God, but it also actively seeks to know and do His will. God, according to John 4:23, seeks true worshipers to worship him.

The faith of Noah caused him to act. God had pronounced judgment on a sinful world (Gen. 6:7) and warned Noah to build an ark (Gen. 6:13-21). The faith of Noah is emphasized because the warning was "of things not seen as yet" (11:7). There were no evidences of an impending storm. Noah had only the word of God. That, however, was enough for Noah. He prepared the vessel which was to become a means of deliverance for himself and his household.

Noah's very act of building the ark "condemned the world" (11:7). As the ark was being constructed, his neighbors would ask concerning its purpose, and he would declare the impending judgment of God upon sinful humanity. Noah exposed himself to ridicule, but he "became heir of the righteousness which is by faith" (11:7).

Abraham, the father of the Israelite nation, shines as one of the greatest men of faith. In answer to the call of God he left Ur of the Chaldees, sojourned for a time at Haran, and then went "into a place which he should after receive for an inheritance" (11:8). Although Canaan was the future home of the patriarch, he did not have any fixed destination there. "By faith he sojourned in the land of promise, as in a strange country" (11:9).

The land was promised to his "seed" or descendants, but Abraham himself did not own one foot of its territory. At the death of Sarah he had to purchase a burial plot from a local Hittite settler (Gen. 23:16).

Abraham, Isaac, and Jacob lived in tents (A.V. "tabernacles") and moved from place to place with their flocks and herds (11:9). Shechem, Bethel, Beer-sheba, Gerar, Hebron—these and other areas were places of temporary settlement. Yet Abraham never found a permanent abode, "for he looked for a city which hath foundations, whose builder and maker is God" (11:10). As a man of faith, Abraham's spiritual sight took him beyond the land of Canaan to the celestial city. He was only a pilgrim below, but he was a citizen of the city of God.

Sarah also enters the line of the faithful (Gen. 17:19; 18:11, 14). Although she laughed at the thought that she could bear a son in her old age, she did believe God (11:11) and received strength from Him for the impossible. It is said of Sarah that "she judged Him faithful who had promised" (11:11).

Because Abraham and his wife Sarah dared to believe God, they became the parents of children "so many as the stars of the sky in multitude, and as the sand which is by the sea shore innumerable" (11:12). Physically, Israel traces its lineage to Abraham. Spiritually, all who are "of faith" look upon Abraham as father. One man's faithfulness produced a rich harvest!

Abraham and the patriarchs "died in faith, not having received the promises, but having seen them afar off" (11:13). God had said to Abraham, "I will make of thee a great nation, and I will bless thee, and make thy name great; . . . and in thee shall all families of the earth be blessed" (Gen. 12:1-3). This was a promise which would not be fulfilled until centuries after the death of the patriarchs. They did not complain, however, but rather rejoiced as they looked to the future. They "confessed that they were strangers and pilgrims on the earth" (11:13; cf. Gen. 23:4).

A man whose sole interest is worldly prosperity will be frustrated if he does not attain it. A man who is content to be a pilgrim here must have a higher goal (11:14). Abraham had known something of the high culture of the Sumerian city of Ur. For centuries Ur had been a center of commerce and cultural activities. It boasted schools and temples. Scribes copied letters and public documents. Artists made fine jewelry. Modern archaeology has helped us to appreciate the meaning of life in Ur during the centuries which preceded Abraham. Yet the patriarch chose to leave it all. Did he ever wish to return? The writer of Hebrews says of the patriarchs, "Truly, if they had been mindful of that country from whence they came out, they might have had opportunity to have returned" (11:15). They chose to leave the great urban centers of their day, and they chose to stay away from them. The reason was that they had something better: "But now they desire a better country, that is, an heavenly" (11:16).

This attitude of faith on the part of the patriarchs evoked a response from God. He "is not ashamed to be called their God" (11:16). This actually became a means of identification. God called himself "the God of Abraham, the God of Isaac, and the God of Jacob" (cf. Exod. 3:6). He also is preparing a city—greater than the earthly Jerusalem—for those who are spiritually ready to inherit it. The Psalmist says, "There is a river, the streams whereof shall make glad the city of our God, the holy place of the tabernacles of the most High" (Ps. 46:4). This is the city "with foundations" for which the patriarchs longed. It is the heavenly country which they so ardently desired.

The greatest trial in Abraham's life came when he was asked to offer his beloved son Isaac as a sacrifice. Abraham had been told, "In Isaac shall thy seed be called" (Gen. 21:12). All of the promises were dependent upon Isaac, who would be expected to grow to maturity and pass them on to his children. If Isaac were to die, God's promises would prove meaningless. Yet Abraham was told to offer Isaac. The aged patriarch prepared to do so (Gen. 22:3), "accounting that God was able to raise him up, even from the dead" (11:19). At the time of the patriarchs, such a miracle would have been unprecedented. Still, Abraham had faith that God would be true to His word under all circumstances. God actually intervened and instructed Abraham to offer a ram caught in a nearby thicket instead of his son Isaac. The child was spared, snatched as it were from the jaws of death by the command of God.

The faith of the patriarchs was frequently evident at the time of their death. Then, with prophetic insight, they looked down the expanse of time and traced the fulfillment of God's purpose. "By faith Isaac blessed Jacob and Esau concerning things to come" (11:20; Gen. 27: 27-40). These blessings were different from those anticipated earlier. Isaac had expected to bestow the blessing of the firstborn on Esau, even though Jacob had earlier sought it from him as the price of a "mess of pottage." With the connivance of Rebekah, Jacob went to his father Isaac and, disguised as Esau, secured the blessing of his father. Subsequently Esau approached his blind father and asked for some blessing. Isaac was grieved at what had been done, but he accepted it as the will of God. A lesser blessing was pronounced on Esau, who became the father of the Edomites, but Jacob became the ancestor of the Israelites, through whom the divine promise continued until it found its fulfillment in the person of Jesus Christ, our Lord. Isaac, by faith, looked down the corridor of time and pronounced blessings on his sons.

Jacob also, at the time of his death, pronounced blessings upon his sons (Gen. 49:2-27). A special blessing was pronounced on the sons of Joseph. Each of Jacob's other sons became fathers of tribes in Israel, but Joseph fathered two tribes, one named after his son Ephraim and the other after Manasseh (Gen. 48:5). Here, too, the elder son was given a second place. Ephraim, the younger, was honored above his brother. By faith Jacob saw the future history of the tribes.

Under similar circumstances, Joseph at the time of his death spoke of the coming exodus. This prophecy came at a time when the Israelites were happily settled in Goshen, long before the time of oppression. Still Joseph insisted that the Israelites not bury him in Egypt: "And Joseph took an oath of the children of Israel, saying, God will surely visit you, and ye shall carry up my bones from hence" (Gen. 50:25). He was subsequently embalmed and placed in a coffin in Egypt, awaiting the exodus.

The parents of Moses exercised faith (11:23) when in

defiance of the king's commandment they hid their infant child. It was the purpose of the Pharaoh to weaken the Israelites by causing the death of the baby boys. Parents were instructed to cast their sons into the Nile River, but the parents of Moses kept him in their home as long as possible and then placed him in an ark of bulrushes in the Nile. There he was found by Pharaoh's daughter, who adopted him and paid the child's mother to act as his nurse.

Moses himself, in adult life, became an excellent example of the life of faith. As the son of Pharaoh's daughter, he had been treated like an Egyptian prince. While his fellow Israelites were suffering, he was going to school in Egypt. Moses might have risen to high rank in the family that adopted him, perhaps even ascending the throne of Egypt. Instead he "refused to be called the son of Pharaoh's daughter; choosing rather to suffer affliction with the people of God, than to enjoy the pleasures of sin for a season" (11:24-25).

The faith of Moses was expressed in a forthright choice. Should he follow the normal course of events, forget his Israelite background, and live the life of a member of Egyptian royalty? The alternative was to become a despised Hebrew slave. By faith Moses chose that alternative. The pleasures of Egypt would last but a short day. Although association with God's people might bring hardship, there was a future with which to reckon.

The choice was between "the reproach of Christ" and the "treasures in Egypt," yet faithful Moses chose Christ (11:26). He considered the rewards of faithfulness to God, and spurned the momentary satisfactions which

fame and position would have given. Had he chosen
otherwise he might well have become a Pharaoh. His
mummified body might be in some museum today. Because he chose to associate himself with the people of
God, he became Israel's lawgiver and the leader of the
exodus, and his name is honored among the great men of
faith. Although he died in the mountains of Moab, he
appeared with Jesus on the Mount of Transfiguration.

It was by faith that Moses "forsook Egypt" (11:27)
after a series of ten plagues on the land. Pharaoh refused to learn that he had to reckon with Israel's God.
Israel was a weak, enslaved nation, yet Moses led that
nation out of the land of bondage. The "wrath of the
king" was aroused. The fleeing Israelites were pursued
by Pharaoh's soldiers, who were destroyed at the Red
Sea. Moses "by faith" undertook an impossible task, but
God was with him. Israel was fed with manna from
Heaven, and drank water from the rock. Their clothing
did not wear out during a generation in the wilderness.
The things that were impossible with men were possible
with God.

The faith of Moses was based on a spiritual principle:
"He endured, as seeing him who is invisible" (11:27).
This is, of course, a paradox. How can one see the invisible? The answer: "With the eye of faith." Peter addressed suffering saints, reminding them of the coming
of the Lord Jesus "Whom, having not seen, ye love; in
whom, though now ye see him not, yet believing ye rejoice with joy unspeakable and full of glory" (I Peter 1:
8). The believer does not insist on seeing God. He walks
"by faith," and in so doing comes to know his Lord in a
personal way. This is what is meant by knowing the love

of Christ, which passes knowledge (Eph. 3:19), and seeing the invisible God.

The tenth plague upon the land of Egypt caused the death of the firstborn of man and beast (Exod. 11:5). Israel, however, was instructed to observe the Passover (11:28; Exod. 12:1-28). Each household was instructed to take a lamb, kill it, and apply the blood to "the two side posts and the upper door post" (Exod. 12:7) of the house. The lamb was eaten by the members of the family and their guests. The blood applied to the house was a guarantee of safety: "And the blood shall be to you for a token upon the house where ye are: and when I see the blood, I will pass over you, and the plague shall not be upon you to destroy you, when I smite the land of Egypt" (Exod. 12:13). Moses, through faith, observed the Passover and thereby brought both protection and deliverance to his people.

When the Israelites reached the Red Sea, they feared they were trapped (Exod. 14:10). The Egyptians were behind them and the sea before them. God instructed Moses to lift his rod (Exod. 14:16) and cause the waters of the sea to be divided. He did so, "and the children of Israel went into the midst of the sea upon the dry ground" (Exod. 14:22). When the enemy sought to follow, "the Lord overthrew the Egyptians in the midst of the sea" (Exod. 14:27). Moses had been willing to trust God in his own life, rejecting the advantages of the Egyptian court. He trusted God as the leader of Israel's exodus. Dark moments were enlightened by God's presence. The faith of Moses was active, however. He not only meditated on the word of God, but he acted upon it.

Acts of faith also marked the entrance of Israel into

Canaan (11:30). The key to the land was the fortress city of Jericho in the Jordan Valley. In obedience to the command of God, the Israelites marched around the city once a day for six days, and seven times on the seventh day (Josh. 6). Then the priests blew their trumpets, the people shouted, and "the wall fell down flat" (Josh. 6: 20). Because of obedience to God, Israel occupied its first stronghold in Canaan.

Within the city of Jericho was a Canaanite woman who showed faith in Israel's God (11:31). When spies first came to the city, before Israel had crossed the Jordan, she said to them, "I know that the Lord hath given you the land" (Josh. 2:9). She had heard of the victories of Joshua's armies east of the Jordan, and she believed in the power of the God of Israel. By faith she had hid the spies, risking her own life. When the city fell to Joshua, Rahab and her family were the only inhabitants who were spared.

Heroes of faith lived during the time of the judges (11:32). Gideon and his three hundred men put to flight the Midianites (Judg. 7:7). Barak, accompanied by Deborah, defeated the northern Canaanites at the River Kishon (Judg. 4-5). Samson, in many ways an unworthy example, called upon God for strength to accomplish the overthrow of the Philistine oppressor: "And Samson said, Let me die with the Philistines. And he bowed himself with all his might; and the house fell upon the lords, and upon all the people that were therein. So the dead which he slew at his death were more than they which he slew in his life" (Judg. 16:30).

Jephthah was another judge whose life was marred by heathen influences. An illegitimate child, he was forced to leave his father's home and dwell among the social outcasts (Judg. 11:1-3). When Israel was threatened by the Ammonites, however, the elders of Gilead sent for Jephthah and offered to make him leader of the tribe if he would lead the armies against the oppressor. Although Jephthah did wrong in vowing to offer as a burnt offering the one who would first come out to meet him on his return after defeating the Ammonites (Judg. 11:30-31), he accomplished the defeat of the enemy through faith in the Lord (Judg. 11:32-33).

Later, during the time of the monarchy, the succession of the faithful continued. David, who had been guilty of grievous sin, was nevertheless a man of faith and was able, under God, to make of Israel a powerful nation. David suffered for his sin. He serves as a reminder that even a man of faith is subject to temptation. The line of the faithful includes Samuel, who anointed Israel's first two kings, and "the prophets" (11:32), those worthies who spoke out for God in a day when people tended to forget His claims upon their lives.

3. *Triumphs of faith,* 11:33-40

The accomplishments of faith are many and varied. Kingdoms arrayed against God's people were subdued. Joshua and the Judges had succeeded in occupying the land of Canaan against insurmountable odds, yet God had brought victory. Sennacherib the Assyrian besieged Jerusalem, yet God saved the city. The men of faith "wrought righteousness," standing for the truth of the Lord in days of spiritual decline. Elijah took his stand with the God of Israel against Ahab and Jezebel and their sinful program of Baal worship, and God gave the

victory. Men of faith "obtained promises," seeing the fulfillment of God's word. Daniel studied the prophecies
of Jeremiah and saw them fulfilled when Cyrus gave the
decree permitting the return of the Israelites to Jerusalem.

Daniel, a man of faith, "stopped the mouths of lions"
(11:33); his companions Shadrach, Meshach, and Abed-
nego were delivered from "the violence of fire" (11:34).
A host of worthies, including David and Elijah, "escaped
the edge of the sword" (11:34). God's servants in Old
Testament times were periodically called upon to wax
"valiant in fight."

The "armies of the aliens" (11:34) have frequently
been arrayed against the people of God, but the man of
faith is not terrorized. Some students think the words
used here have particular reference to the victories of the
Maccabees over the Syrian forces of Antiochus Epi-
phanes.

The Bible speaks of women who "received their dead
raised to life again" (11:35). Elijah restored a son to
the widow of Zarephath (I Kings 17:17), and Elisha
brought back to life the Shunamite's son (II Kings 4:32-
37). Some of God's people, however, "were tortured, not
accepting deliverance; that they might obtain a better
resurrection" (11:35). Such were the martyrs who were
offered liberty if they would deny their faith. But they
chose to die, honoring God. Death did not come to all,
however. Some lived amid "cruel mockings and scourg-
ings, yea, moreover, of bonds and imprisonment" (11:
36). This was true of Jeremiah, who was placed in the
stocks by Pashur (Jer. 20:2).

Death by stoning (11:37) was the fate of Naboth,

whose desire to keep the inheritance which he had received from his fathers was an offence to Jezebel (I Kings 21:1-14). Tradition suggests that Isaiah was "sawn asunder" during the idolatrous rule of Manasseh. Hundreds of the Lord's prophets were "slain with the sword" by the order of wicked Jezebel (I Kings 19:10).

Many of the godly lacked the bare necessities of life: "they wandered about in sheepskins and goatskins; being destitute, afflicted, tormented" (11:37). Such were Elijah (I Kings 19:13), as he fled from Ahab, and David, as he sought refuge from Saul, who was determined to kill him. Such men willingly turned their backs on the comforts of life because of their high regard for spiritual realities. They could have lived a "normal" life, but they refused to compromise with evil. There is a rightness in the removal of such people from the world, for indeed "the world was not worthy" (11:38) of them. The world is moving along with its own standard of values, but these men lived for better and more enduring things. Deserts, mountains, dens, and caves of the earth (11:38) are no real burden to the man of faith. His life is centered in spiritual realities, and things of time and sense are quite secondary.

Those who have gone ahead, whether martyrs or faithful men who lived out their life span, had one thing in common. Although they "had a good report through faith" (11:39), they "received not the promise." They died without having personally entered into the realization of that which had been promised. They, like Moses, viewed the promised land from afar.

It was not God's purpose to bring about the consummation "without us" (11:40). The Old Testament saints looked, by faith, to the day of Messiah's coming and kingdom. Until that day came, they could not enter into their full reward. The New Covenant is "better" than the Old. The door of grace is opened to Jew and Gentile alike. At the appearing of Jesus, the hopes of Old Testament saints and New Testament saints alike shall be realized. Sufferings and privations will have given way to glory. Perfection will come when we see Him of whom both Old Testament and New Testament speak, the Saviour from sin, Who will reign as King of kings and Lord of lords.

E. RUNNING THE RACE, 12:1-3

The faithful Christian is not alone. Although he may feel destitute, he is assured of the continuing presence of God Himself, Who has promised never to leave or forsake His own. The Christian knows, however, that he is also a part of an army of faithful servants of God. Many of these have lived in days gone by. Luther, Calvin, Knox, Wesley, Moody—these and countless others were faithful to the sacred trust committed unto them in their generation. We go back farther, however, to the worthies mentioned in Hebrews 11. These, whose lives are known to us from the Bible, were also men subject to like passions as we are (James 5:17). We are one with them, as with the saints of all ages.

As an incentive to faithfulness, the author of Hebrews reminds us that we are "compassed about" with a great cloud of witnesses (12:1). The description is graphic. We are in the arena. The race has begun. The witnesses are watching. Delitzsch observes: "Once witnesses for God, they now are witnesses of us, their brethren: the two notions are closely intertwined. Our life here is a contest, its theater the universe, the seats of the spectators are ranged through heaven."

We should observe that there is no explicit statement here or elsewhere in Scripture that the saints who have gone to glory know what is going on in this world. Arguments pro and con are all from silence. God has not seen fit to reveal that detail concerning His children who have entered His presence. We are told, however, that they are with the Lord, they surround us like spectators in an arena, and their example of faithfulness in their respective generations should be an incentive to us to be faithful in ours.

The imagery of the arena continues as the Christian life is likened to a race which must be run. It is, of course, only the Christian who runs. The gift of life is a prerequisite to the ability to take part in a race. Yet all do not use the gift of life in the best way. There are rewards for faithfulness which may be missed.

The preparation for the race is all-important. We must lay aside "weights" (12:1). The illustration is intentionally ridiculous. What runner would think of carrying weights? Everything superfluous must be put aside if he hopes to win. So it is with the Christian. Sometimes we ask, "Is such-and-such a sin?" There may be instances where opinions will differ. Some things are known to be evil, and others may be on the borderline. The Christian must ask a further question, however: "Are they weights?" If they will slow our pace in running the race set before us, then they must be cast aside.

There are also besetting sins which must be cast away. The Christian never gets beyond the reach of temptation.

The evil one is subtle. One man will be ensnared with the lust of the flesh, and the pride of life may be the besetting sin of another. Jealousy, envy, and greed ensnare some who would not fall prey to drunkenness or gluttony. Lack of faith may be the sin to which all of us are prone. By God's grace we are called upon to cast it away. True, we cannot gain the victory alone, yet our Lord has commanded us to remove all that hinders. In bold language Jesus said, "If thy right eye offend thee, pluck it out . . . if thy right hand offend thee, cut it off" (Matt. 5:29-30). Jesus was not hinting that evil exists in things or that the removal of physical organs would make us holier people. He was emphatically teaching, however, that nothing should be so dear and precious to us that we would hold on to it if it were an offense. Sins and weights must go if we are to run the race.

The race is to be run "with patience" (12:1). The need of effort and hard work need not be minimized, but special emphasis must be placed on patience. The Hebrews to whom the letter was addressed had suffered and were growing impatient. "Why doesn't God do something?" is a question we can't always answer. It is enough to know that He knows the beginning and the end, that He has all power, and that He is the God of all grace. We have trusted a faithful Creator and Redeemer.

During the race it is necessary to have the attention focused upon the goal: "Looking unto Jesus the author and finisher of our faith" (12:2). If we look to our fellow runners we will surely be slowed down. What others do is not our concern save, of course, as we seek to encourage them in their Christian testimony. They are not our guide or standard. Our Saviour alone is that. He is the Author of our faith. Our very life has come from Him. He is also its Finisher. Paul could testify, "I know whom I have believed, and am persuaded that he is able to keep that which I have committed unto him against that day" (II Tim. 1:12).

A new insight into the sufferings of the Son of God is given in the words, "Who for the joy that was set before him endured the cross, despising the shame, and is set down at the right hand of the throne of God" (12:2). Why did Jesus endure the agonies of Calvary? Why was He willing to be forsaken of the Father? The answer is majestic in its simplicity. He had a loving purpose. The joy of redeeming His people made Him willing to endure the Cross. The agonies of Calvary cannot be minimized. There Jesus paid the ransom price for His people. But they were people He loved. He did not enter the valley of death in a grudging mood. No man took his life from Him. He gave it willingly, even joyfully, in order to redeem us! This is grace enough to leave all of us speechless.

F. SUFFERINGS AS DISCIPLINE, 12:4-11

Hebrews makes a practical application of this great truth to a generation which had grown indifferent. Christ had to meet the jeers of sinful men (12:3). When you are tempted to waver, remember Him! Sinners actually demanded His life and, as a result of their godless demands, Pontius Pilate delivered Him up to be crucified. The readers of the Epistle to the Hebrews had "not yet resisted unto blood" (12:4), although they might one day become martyrs. Were they willing to pay the price of discipleship? The Christian life is a battle, "striving against sin." In every battle there are casualties.

The Hebrews are also charged with forgetfulness. God had said, "My son, despise not thou the chastening of the Lord, nor faint when thou art rebuked of him" (12:5; Prov. 3:11-12). This is a word addressed to children. It is given in an environment of love. Chastening is actually a mark of sonship (12:7). A father does not chastise strangers, but his own sons are subject to the discipline of his household. A lack of chastening on the part of God the Father might be interpreted as evidence that we were not truly born into the family of God (12:8).

Earthly fathers are, of course, fallible. They may lack proper judgment in the discipline they enforce. Nevertheless we recognize their responsibilities as fathers and honor them for the provisions they make for the discipline of their children. God, however, is the Father of spirits, the Creator of all things. How much more should we accord honor and reverence to Him for His divine government (12:9)!

Human fathers chastise children in order that they may become honorable, productive members of the household. There may appear a tinge of selfishness in this at times, although the child is helped to take his proper place in the family. The chastisement of God is always "for our profit, that we might be partakers of his holiness" (12:10). God has every right to ask service of His children. His discipline, however, has no admixture of selfishness within it. He seeks our good and knows that trials produce strength of character.

Such remarks may seem unduly pious to the individual who is suffering. He may insist that the hardship which he is experiencing is "grievous" (12:11). The answer recognizes that fact. It is in the nature of chastisements to be unpleasant. God's children may go through excruciatingly painful experiences. God has not promised to save His children from the fiery furnace, but He has promised to be with them in their time of need. The chastisement is hard to endure, but God will give the grace of endurance. The Christian can accept it with thanks because of its results: "Nevertheless afterward it yieldeth the peaceable fruit of righteousness unto them which are exercised thereby" (12:11). The believer knows that God knows what He is doing.

G. DUTIES TOWARD THE BRETHREN, 12:12-17

Discouraged believers are encouraged to steadfastness. Quoting Isaiah 35:3 and Proverbs 4:26, the author urged: "Wherefore lift up the hands which hang down, and the feeble knees; and make straight paths for your feet, lest that which is lame be turned out of the way; but let it rather be healed" (12:12-13). The picture is one of gloom. The people are discouraged because of a series of adversities. They are encouraged to renewed life and activity, however. God has not forgotten them. The weak can be made strong. Let the lame be healed and join the battle again!

Another exhortation needed by the Hebrews was in the area of human relations: "Follow peace with all men" (12:14). Discouragement breeds disharmony. Christian was suspicious of Christian, and each felt that he had a particularly heavy burden to bear. A true spiritual revival always results in strained relationships being rectified and believers esteeming one another as fellow members of the Body of Christ.

Peace and holiness are coupled together (12:14). A right relation with fellow believers should accompany a right relation to God. Actually the two ideas are very closely related: "And this commandment have we from him, That he who loveth God love his brother also" (I John 4:21). When a man comes to know Christ, he becomes a new creature and a member of the household of faith. He becomes a "saint," one who is separated to Christ, although he may not always behave in a saintly way. This holiness, imparted to the believer, marks him as different from the worldling. The believer, of course, has the capacity to grow in God's grace, and become more Christlike day by day. Apart, however, from that initial holy nature, the mark of a Christian, a man is but a professor and shall not "see the Lord" (12:14).

Each believer is called upon to exercise a spiritual concern for his fellow Christians (12:15). Is there a lack of manifestation of God's grace in the lives of believers? Are there evidences of a bitter spirit in the church? (Cf. Deut. 29:18.) Such bitterness, unchecked, will result in apostasy.

One such example may be cited from the Old Testament. Esau was the firstborn son of Isaac and might have become his father's chief heir. He was, however, a "fornicator" (12:16). This expression is probably an allusion to the fact that he married "Hittite" wives to the sorrow of his parents. This was evidence of a lack of spiritual discernment, for his father and grandfather had been called to turn their backs on heathenism and live lives of faithful witness to the God of Israel. Esau is also

described as a "profane" man. The term has no reference
to his speech but to the secular nature of his life. He
lived for the things of this world. We cannot excuse
Jacob for taking unfair advantage of Esau, but we note
that hungry Esau persuaded himself that the birthright
would do him no good if he starved to death. He could
not trust God to meet his needs. For "one morsel of
meat" he "sold his birthright" (12:16).

There is no record of any great sin in Esau's life. He
was a moral but wholly secular man. Isaac desired to
convey the blessing to Esau, but Rebekah joined Jacob
in fooling his blind father. After Jacob was blessed,
Esau came to his father and sought a blessing. But it had
already been given. Esau recognized the value of the
birthright after it was too late. His tears could not bring
it back to him (12:17).

H. The Two Covenants, 12:18-29

The believer today approaches God through Jesus
Christ. The Old Testament, however, presented a God
who was holy and remote from His people. The experiences at Mount Sinai graphically illustrate this. Sinai
was a "mount that might be touched" (12:18), i.e. a material mountain. The giving of the Law there was accompanied by natural manifestations of terrific power—vol-
canic fire, blackness, gloom, and a tempest (perhaps a
whirlwind) (Exod. 20:18-20). God was showing His
sovereign power and infinite holiness to a people who
had to learn their need of His saving grace. This was
one of the "diverse manners" in which God spoke in the
Old Testament (cf. Heb. 1:1).

Israel at Sinai heard the blast of a trumpet followed by

the proclamation of God's Law (12:19). Condemned, the people asked that the voice be silenced. Not even a beast could approach the mountain (12:20), and Moses himself said, "I exceedingly fear and quake" (12:21). The thunderings of Sinai proclaimed the holiness of God and the sinfulness of His people. None could abide in the presence of the Almighty (cf. Deut. 9:19).

The Christian may compare New Testament Sion (Zion) with Old Testament Sinai. Zion is a name which was applied to Jerusalem, the holy city. Here the Temple was built, and here Jesus was crucified. From a hill east of the city He ascended to Heaven. The earthly "city of God" was but a reflection of the heavenly Jerusalem (12:22), the abode of angels and the saints of all ages (12:23).

The Christian approaches God, "the Judge of all" (12:23), and Jesus, "the mediator of the new covenant." The atoning blood of Jesus may be contrasted with the shed blood of Abel, the first martyr. The blood of Abel called for vengeance and was witness to man's guilt. The blood of Jesus, however, calls for pardon. It is witness to God's love for guilty men. Abel, and all martyrs, should be honored for their testimony to the truth. Jesus should be worshiped as the divine Redeemer.

Although Sinai and Zion may be contrasted, both speak of the same God, whose character never changes. Those who refused to hear His word from Sinai met a fearful judgment (12:25). As the Son speaks a word of grace from Heaven, He, too, has the right to be heard. To turn from Him is to court disaster.

When God manifested Himself to Moses and the Is-

raelites, "the whole mount quaked greatly" (Exod. 19:
18). The prophet Haggai depicted a future day when God
would shake "the heavens, and the earth, and the sea,
and the dry land" (Hag. 2:6). The author of Hebrews
used these "shakings" as a symbol of the end of the old
order. Everything that can be shaken has been shaken
(12:26-27). The old order, including the Temple worship with its Levitical offerings, is now past. All that is
of the earth is shaken in order to make room for a kingdom which "cannot be shaken" (Heb. 12:27). Christ's
session at the right hand of the Father, His intercessory
ministry in a heavenly sanctuary—these are heavenly realities unrelated to the world of change and decay. Those
who look to the earthly structures will suffer disappoint-
ment. Look above to the heavenly reality! This is the
exhortation of Hebrews.

There is a practical response to this. Although we cannot "build" the heavenly city—God has done that—still
we can offer grateful service to the God of our salvation.
He is not a God different in character from the God of
Sinai. He must be approached with reverence (12:28).
He is a consuming fire (12:29) to those who despise His
mercy. He is, however, the God who sent His Son to die
for sinners and the God who takes no delight in the death
of the wicked. If the God of Sinai and of Zion is the
same, the mountains themselves speak of different realities. Sinai says, "Stand afar off." When Jesus died, the
veil of the Temple in Jerusalem was parted so that anyone could enter the Holy of Holies. Zion says, "Enter,
through the new and living way consecrated for you
through the blood of the Saviour."

I. CHRISTIAN DUTIES, 13:1-17

1. *Moral and social relations,* 13:1-6

The Epistle to the Hebrews closes, as do the Pauline letters, with a series of practical, often personal, injunctions. The Christian life, lived in the power of the Spirit of God, should be a means of blessing and encouragement to others. The Christian should be marked by brotherly love (13:1). Actually we would do well to speak of "brother love," for Christians are related to one another as members of Christ and children of God through faith in Him.

The grace of hospitality was appreciated in the ancient world where it was often a necessity. In the absence of hotels and YMCA's it was the responsibility of the individual to care for the needs of the wayfarer. "I was a stranger, and ye took me in" (Matt. 25:35), is an expression of gratitude for hospitality. When strangers passed the door of Abraham (Gen. 18), he made careful preparation to feed and care for them. Unwittingly he had "entertained angels unawares" (13:2).

It is true, of course, that we are not able to extend the indiscriminate hospitality in our culture that was observed by the Biblical patriarchs. The principles, however, still abide. It is our privilege to entertain the Lord's servants as they move about. What a blessing to have a home in which pastors and missionaries are always welcomed! If we do not have ample facilities to care for guests and there are facilities in local hotels, we should certainly be ready to help care for the expenses of entertaining the Lord's servants there.

Some, however, will be concerned about the true

stranger—one who may not even be a Christian. Do we have a responsibility to him? Frequently we will be the only "gospel" he will ever read. Helpfulness may not always mean giving money or lodging. To give money to a drunkard may help confirm him in his sinful habit. The Christian will, however, always reckon that he is his brother's keeper. The readiness always to lend a helping hand should be the mark of all who profess to be disciples of Jesus, of whom it is written that He "went about doing good" (Acts 10:38).

A further responsibility of the Christian was the sympathetic visitation of prisoners. Many were imprisoned because of their faith in Christ. Christians who were not so imprisoned were to consider themselves one with their afflicted brethren (13:3). There was always the possibility that the man who was free one day might be imprisoned the next. Those "in the body" had every reason to expect persecution. This should have proved a stimulus to a sympathetic appreciation of their suffering brethren.

It has only been in recent decades that prisons provided ample food, shelter, and medical care for their inmates. Paul, in II Timothy, explains his needs while in a prison near the Roman forum. Luke, the beloved physician, was with him (II Tim. 4:11), but the apostle was evidently cold and wanted the cloak which he had left in Troas (II Tim. 4:13). There was a degree of urgency, for Paul wrote, "Do thy diligence to come shortly unto me" (II Tim. 4:9). Christians were frequently persecuted by the Roman Empire during the first three centuries of the Christian Church. The Christian was not to be surprised at this, but he was to support his fellow in times of need.

The Christian attitude toward marriage (13:4) indicates the purity which was expected of true disciples. The institution of marriage is of divine origin and is to be held to be honorable by all. The procreation of children has been ordained by God, and all who would find fault with its legitimate expression within the bonds of marriage are guilty of finding fault with the Creator. The immoral man and the adulterer, however, is in a different category. Sexual distinctions have been made by God for the accomplishment of His will. The violation of the marriage relationship, however, is a sin in the sight of God. Those who are guilty "God will judge" (13:4).

The life of the Christian is to be free from covetousness (13:5). The word translated "without covetousness" means, literally, "not-money-loving." There is a right and a wrong use of money. Money may be used properly by those who are faithful stewards of the trust which God has committed to them. Money also may be abused by those who make it an end in itself or a means to ends which do not glorify God. Covetousness is a sure sign of discontent. It impiles a lack of trust in God. His promise, "I will never leave thee, nor forsake thee," should satisfy us in our moments of fear (13:5). The Christian is never left to his own resources. He can say, "The Lord is my helper, and I will not fear what man shall do unto me" (13:6).

2. *Loyalty to leaders in the Church,* 13:7-8

Although recognizing but one High Priest, Jesus Christ, the "author and finisher" of our faith, the Christian is exhorted to give due honor to God's servants who have been placed in positions of responsibility in the Church. The risen Christ "gave some, apostles; and some, prophets; and some, evangelists; and some, pastors and teachers; for the perfecting of the saints, for the work of the ministry, for the edifying of the body of Christ" (Eph. 4:11-12). The author of Hebrews exhorts, "Remember them which have the rule over you" (13:7). They have been placed there by God and are to be honored as God's servants. Their example of faithfulness is to be followed by those to whom they minister.

The faith of the Christian leaders is summarized in one line: "Jesus Christ the same yesterday, and to day, and for ever" (13:8). The Christian is in a world of change. The social structure of the first century A.D. saw mighty changes. Jerusalem was conquered and the Temple destroyed. Our generation has been threatened with extinction by missiles which can bring instant destruction to millions. Is there anything that is eternally the same? The Christian answers, "Jesus Christ." His kingdom cannot be moved. He is the foundation on which to build, a rock which will remain firm when the shifting sands of earth have proved a false hope.

3. *Warning against heresies,* 13:9-14

The Christian is continually tempted to look to "divers and strange doctrines" (13:9). The individuals to whom the epistle was addressed were tempted to go back to a form of Judaism, specifically the Old Testament ordinances regarding food and drink. Such observances, they are warned (13:9), have not really benefited those who observe them. The heart is strengthened by God's grace, not by foods!

At the time of the writing of Hebrews there were still two altars—one in the Jerusalem Temple, and one in Heaven. Trust might be put in the efficacy of one or the other, but it was impossible to trust both. Those who serve in the Tabernacle have no right to eat of our altar (13:10), the writer insists. The Christian altar is in Heaven, where Christ serves as priest.

An analogy may be drawn, however, between the ritual of the Day of Atonement and the position of Christians in the first century. The body of the animal used by the High Priest as a sin offering was burned outside the camp (Lev. 16:27). As a matter of historic fact, Jesus also, rejected by His people, died beyond the walls of Jerusalem, "outside the camp" of the Judaism of His day (13:12). This being so, the writer urges his readers, "Let us go forth therefore unto him without the camp, bearing his reproach" (13:13). It is no disgrace to be with Jesus, outside the camp. If the unbeliever threatens to excommunicate you, do not be fearful. Gladly join your Lord and Redeemer.

Rejection by the "camp" is really no great tragedy. In this world we have "no continuing city" (13:14). We will be pilgrims and strangers as long as we are here, but we do have a heavenly citizenship. We seek the city that is to come, and we live for the day when the Saviour shall return for His bride! We will, of course, seek so to conduct ourselves here that we may glorify our Lord. Our roots are not here, however. Our earthly possessions must be left behind, but we have treasures in Heaven, where moth and rust do not corrupt, and thieves do not break through and steal.

4. *Life in the Church,* 13:15-17

The citizen of the heavenly city has one offering to make. The blood of bulls and goats is no longer necessary now that Jesus has offered Himself as our substitute. We bring, however, "the sacrifice of praise" (13:15). This is described as "the fruit of our lips" (cf. Hosea 14: 2). The great motive of Christian living is thanks to God. The sacrifice of our great High Priest was once, for all, but our praise is to be offered "continually."

Our praise finds further expression in lives of Christian love: "To do good and to communicate forget not: for with such sacrifices God is well pleased" (13:16). The word rendered "communicate" (*koinonia*) suggests sharing with needy brethren. The Christian gives praise to God, and he shares his material goods with brethren who lack this world's goods. Some Christians lost all their property during times of persecution, but others gladly shared—sometimes from their poverty—because of the grace of God in their lives.

Earlier (13:7), the Hebrews had been exhorted to remember their spiritual leaders and continue steadfast in their faith. Now (13:17) they are told to obey them. The church leaders have a solemn responsibility for the souls of those entrusted to them by God. One day they shall give an account of their stewardship before the Lord. The accounting will be joyous if the members of the church have been faithful in Christian life and witness, but it will be sad if there are those who have denied the faith or have become carnal in their lives.

Although the doctrine of individual responsibility before God is often stressed in Scripture, we are not to conclude that the Christian may live a life of lawlessness
with respect to others. The Church is the body through
which the Lord normally works, and its leaders are to
be given due honor. If they become hirelings and deny
the Lord who bought them, they must be rejected. Normally, however, the church member should pray for and
encourage his pastor as a man of God. The pastor must
identify himself with his people and seek their spiritual
welfare even at times when his concern seems resented.
On one occasion Paul had to say, "I will very gladly
spend and be spent for you; though the more abundantly
I love you, the less I be loved" (II Cor. 12:15).

J. Personal Matters, 13:18-25

1. *A request for prayer*, 13:18-19

The writer of the epistle closes with a number of personal requests. He asks an interest in the prayers of the
people (13:18), for he has lived before them in all hon-
esty, seeking their spiritual good as a faithful servant of
Jesus Christ. He longs to see them again and wants them
to pray that he will soon be restored to fellowship with
them (13:19).

2. *Prayer for the Church*, 13:20-21

The apostle, in turn, prayed for the people. His prayer
is frequently, and appropriately, used as a benediction.
It begins by addressing "the God of peace" (13:20). In
an hour when many believers were being persecuted and
some were wavering in their faith, it was well to be reminded that God is a God of peace. Peace for the soul

has been provided by the sacrifice of Christ on Calvary, and the mind may enjoy peace as it is stayed on Him.

The great act which guarantees our peace for time and eternity is next mentioned in this benediction. He "brought again from the dead our Lord Jesus, that great shepherd of the sheep" (13:20). Sheep tend to wander, but Jesus is the Good Shepherd who seeks His sheep until He finds them. This Shepherd died for His sheep, but He is alive and, as the Good Shepherd, still loves His flock.

The sheep are safe because the Shepherd shed "the blood of the everlasting covenant." The Sinai Covenant was temporal, but the New Covenant in the blood of Jesus is eternal. Those who belong to Him have eternal life. They are eternally secure.

The benediction continues with a prayer for a work of God in the hearts of those to whom the letter was addressed. God's will is supreme, and the Christian properly prays for the accomplishment of God's will. It is the highest form of prayer to pray, "Thy will be done." Here the writer prays that the Hebrews may be equipped ("make . . . perfect") with everything necessary to do God's will. We must remember that sinful man cannot of himself do that which is pleasing to God. Sin permeates our being, but the Spirit of God can so direct and empower us that we shall be able to gain victory over sin and do His will. That which is "wellpleasing in His sight" is, in the last analysis, that which is best for all men. If God works within us to do His will, we are blessed indeed.

The benediction closes by reminding us that all of God's work is "through Jesus Christ; to whom be glory for ever and ever" (13:21). He is the Lord of glory. In humiliation He took upon Himself our sinful nature and suffered the death of the cross. He is, however, the risen and glorified Lord, to whom angels and archangels ascribe praise along with the redeemed of all ages.

3. *A request to be heard,* 13:22-23

As a final personal note, the writer urges his readers to "suffer the word of exhortation" (13:22). He could have written more about their temptations and dangers, but he has tried to be brief. The words come from a heart of love, and he hopes they will be received in that spirit. Timothy has just been set free (presumably from prison). The writer of the letter, in referring to Timothy, shows himself to have been a member of the Pauline circle. Timothy will probably accompany the writer of the epistle to visit the readers (at Rome?) soon.

4. *Greetings and grace,* 13:24-25

The writer sends his greetings to the leaders of the church (13:24), whom he evidently knows very well. The letter itself had highly commended them to the wavering Christians. "They of Italy salute you" could mean either that the writer was in Italy when he wrote the letter, or that he was away from Italy, addressing a letter to Christians there, and that people from Italy who were in the city when the letter was written sent their greetings to countrymen back home. The latter seems to have been the case.

The letter closes with a final brief greeting: "Grace be with you all. Amen" (13:25). All of the mercies of God flow forth from His grace.

BIBLIOGRAPHY

ARCHER, GLEASON L. *The Epistle to the Hebrews.* Grand Rapids: Baker Book House, 1957.

CHADWICK, G. A. *The Epistle to the Hebrews.* London: Religious Tract Society, n.d.

DAVIDSON, A. B. *The Epistle to the Hebrews.* Grand Rapids: Zondervan Publishing House, 1950.

DELITZSCH, FRANZ. *Commentary on the Epistle to the Hebrews.* Grand Rapids: Wm. B. Eerdmans Publishing Company, 1952 (reprint).

HEWITT, THOMAS. *The Epistle to the Hebrews.* Grand Rapids: Wm. B. Eerdmans Publishing Co., 1960.

LANG, G. H. *The Epistle to the Hebrews.* London: Paternoster Press, 1951.

LENSKI, R. C. H. *The Interpretation of the Epistle to the Hebrews and of the Epistle of James.* Columbus, Ohio: The Wartburg Press, 1937.

MALL, CARL BERNHARD. *The Epistle to the Hebrews,* A. C. Kendrick, Tr., Lange Commentary Series. New York: Charles Scribners' Sons, 1868.

MOFFATT, JAMES. *A Critical and Exegetical Commentary on the Epistle to the Hebrews.* Edinburgh: T. & T. Clark, 1924.

NEIL, WILLIAM. *The Epistle to the Hebrews.* London: S. C. M. Press, 1955.

Newell, William R. *Hebrews Verse by Verse*. Chicago: Moody Press, 1947.

Pink, Arthur W. *An Exposition of Hebrews*. Swengel, Pa.: Bible Truth Depot, 1954.

Robinson, Theodore H. *The Epistle to the Hebrews*. London: Hodder and Stoughton, 1933.

Saphir, Adolph. *The Epistle to the Hebrews*. New York: Loizeaux Bros., n.d.

Thomas, W. H. Griffith. *Let Us Go On*. Grand Rapids: Zondervan Publishing House, 1944.

Vos, Geerhardus. *The Teaching of the Epistle to the Hebrews*. Grand Rapids: Wm. B. Eerdmans Publishing Company, 1956.

Westcott, B. F. *The Epistle to the Hebrews*. Grand Rapids: Wm. B. Eerdmans Publishing Company, 1950 (reprint).

Wuest, Kenneth S. *Hebrews in the Greek New Testament*. Grand Rapids: Wm. B. Eerdmans Publishing Company, 1948.

Moody Press, a ministry of the Moody Bible Institute, is designed for education, evangelization and edification. If we may assist you in knowing more about Christ and the Christian life, please write us without obligation to: Moody Press, c/o MLM, Chicago, Illinois 60610.